Regional Mitigation Strategy for the Dry Lake Solar Energy Zone

Produced by:
Bureau of Land Management
March 2014

ACKNOWLEDGMENTS

This technical note is the product of a collaborative effort. Many people representing many different entities had a hand in its development. The project occurred under the leadership of Ray Brady, Bureau of Land Management (BLM) Washington Office. The final content was approved by the BLM Regional Mitigation Project Team: Joe Vieira (Lead), Michael Dwyer, Wendy Seley, and Gordon Toevs. Special thanks go to the Argonne National Laboratory project support team: Heidi Hartmann (Lead), Laura Fox, David Murphy, Karen Smith, Shannon Stewart, Konstance Wescott, and Lee Walston. Special thanks also go to John McCarty (BLM Washington Office), Rochelle Francisco (BLM Nevada State Office), Fred Edwards, Mark Slaughter, Kathleen Sprowl, Boris Poff, and the other members of the BLM Southern Nevada District, Pahrump Field Office Interdisciplinary Team.

Members of the Information and Publishing Services Section at the BLM National Operations Center assisted by providing editorial and design and layout services. Many others contributed by attending or helping conduct one or more of the workshops conducted to obtain input from interested parties, by providing comments on draft versions of this document, and by providing management oversight and/or technical support. Thanks to all who contributed!

TABLE OF CONTENTS

Figures

Tables

The "Regional Mitigation Strategy for the Dry Lake Solar Energy Zone" presents a strategy for compensating for the unavoidable impacts that are expected from the development of the Dry Lake Solar Energy Zone (SEZ) in southern Nevada. This strategy responds to a call for the development of solar regional mitigation strategies for each of the SEZs, as committed to in the record of decision for the "Final Programmatic Environmental Impact Statement (PEIS) for Solar Energy Development in Six Southwestern States." The strategy consists of preliminary findings and recommendations for conducting each element of a process that identifies: (1) the unavoidable impacts of utility-scale solar development in the Dry Lake SEZ that may warrant regional mitigation; (2) mitigation actions that can be implemented in the region to compensate for those impacts; (3) how a regional mitigation fee could be calculated; and (4) how the impacts and mitigation actions could be monitored. While this pilot strategy for the Dry Lake SEZ is not a Bureau of Land Management decision, it will inform future decision documents for: configuration of lease parcels within the Dry Lake SEZ; lease stipulations; impacts to be mitigated in the region; where and how regional mitigation will occur; and how monitoring and adaptive management will occur.

1.1 Purpose of the Strategy

The "Regional Mitigation Strategy for the Dry Lake Solar Energy Zone" recommends a strategy for compensating for certain unavoidable impacts that are expected from the development of the Dry Lake Solar Energy Zone (SEZ) in southern Nevada. The Bureau of Land Management (BLM) is required to manage the public lands in a manner that will protect the quality of ecological and environmental values and provide for wildlife habitat in a way that does not result in the permanent impairment of the productivity of the land. While the BLM places a priority on mitigating impacts to an acceptable level onsite, there are times when onsite mitigation alone may not be sufficient. In these cases, which are likely to occur with utility-scale solar development, which often involves a long-term commitment of resources over a relatively large area, the BLM is considering requirements for regional mitigation for those unavoidable impacts that could exacerbate problematic regional trends. Accordingly, this pilot strategy articulates:

1. The unavoidable impacts expected as a result of development of the Dry Lake SEZ.

2. The problematic trends in the Mojave Desert, where the Dry Lake SEZ is located.

3. A conceptual model that depicts the relationships between resources, ecosystem functions, ecosystem services, and change agents (including development, climate change, wildfire, etc.).

4. The unavoidable impacts that, in consideration of regional trends and roles the impacted resources play, may warrant regional mitigation.

5. The regional mitigation goals and objectives recommended for the Dry Lake SEZ.

6. The regional mitigation locations and action(s) recommended for achieving the mitigation goals and objectives for the Dry Lake SEZ.

7. The estimated cost of the mitigation action(s), including a breakout of acquisition, restoration, and/or ongoing management costs to ensure effectiveness and durability.

8. A recommended method for calculating a mitigation fee that could be assessed to developers and an explanation of how it was calculated for the Dry Lake SEZ.

9. A recommendation for how the BLM fee revenue derived from development of the Dry Lake SEZ could be managed.

10. A recommendation for how the outcomes of the mitigation actions could be monitored and what will happen if the actions are not achieving the desired results.

This pilot strategy will guide future decisions for:

- The configuration of lease parcels within the Dry Lake SEZ.
- The lease stipulations to achieve avoidance and minimization of impacts.
- The impacts to be mitigated in the immediate region.
- Where and how regional mitigation will occur.
- Monitoring and adaptive management.
- Developing BLM policy to guide regional mitigation.

The BLM authorized officer will make these decisions prior to leasing and will also take into consideration:

- The National Environmental Policy Act (NEPA) analysis done for the proposed action, including comments submitted by the public and other stakeholders.
- Any changes to the applicable resource management plan (RMP) or other plans that affect management of the SEZ or possible mitigation sites.
- The input received from consultation with tribes.
- Any other information that would update, correct, or otherwise supplement the information contained in this strategy.

1.2 Background

In 2012, the BLM and the U.S. Department of Energy published the "Final Programmatic Environmental Impact Statement (PEIS) for Solar Energy Development in Six Southwestern States" (Final Solar PEIS). The Final Solar PEIS assessed the impact of utility-scale solar energy development on public lands in the six southwestern states of Arizona, California, Colorado, Nevada, New Mexico, and Utah. The "Approved Resource Management Plan Amendments/ Record of Decision (ROD) for Solar Energy Development in Six Southwestern States" (Solar PEIS ROD) implemented a comprehensive solar energy program for public lands in those states and incorporated land use allocations and programmatic and SEZ-specific design features into land use plans in the six-state study area (BLM 2012). The Solar PEIS ROD identified 17 priority areas for utility-scale solar energy development, or SEZs. The Final Solar PEIS presents a detailed analysis of the expected impacts of solar development on each SEZ.

Comments on both the Draft Solar PEIS and the Supplement to the Draft Solar PEIS encouraged the BLM to incorporate a robust mitigation framework into the proposed solar energy program to address unavoidable impacts expected in SEZs. In the Supplement to the Draft Solar PEIS, the BLM presented, as part of its incentives for SEZs, the concept of regional mitigation planning[1]. A draft framework for regional mitigation planning was posted on the project web page between the publication of the Supplement to the Draft Solar PEIS and the Final Solar PEIS to foster stakeholder engagement. A framework for regional mitigation planning was included in the Final Solar PEIS and the Solar PEIS ROD. Concurrent with the development of this strategy, the BLM has developed a technical reference, titled "Procedural Guidance for Developing Solar Regional Mitigation Strategies," to provide guidance on the process and a refined framework to aid in the preparation of solar regional mitigation strategies (SRMSs) for other SEZs (BLM forthcoming).

The BLM's policy is to mitigate impacts to an acceptable level onsite whenever possible through avoidance, minimization, remediation, or reduction of impacts over time. The use of regional mitigation is evaluated by the BLM on a case-by-case basis and is based on the need to address resource issues that cannot be acceptably mitigated onsite. Furthermore, not all adverse impacts can or must be fully mitigated either onsite or in the immediate region. A certain level of adverse or unavoidable impact may be acceptable: (1) when an appropriate level of mitigation will be conducted and remaining impacts do not result in unnecessary or undue degradation; or (2) when impacts to BLM sensitive species or Endangered Species Act-listed species do not exceed established resource and value objectives.

In order to minimize the impacts of solar development, the BLM applies a mitigation hierarchy, consisting of avoid, minimize, and compensate. Implementation of this hierarchy begins with the location and configuration of the SEZs, so as to avoid as many conflicts as possible. Avoidance is also used within the boundaries of SEZs by designating nondevelopable areas. Minimization involves the implementation of design features (which are required mitigation measures) and management practices meant to reduce the impacts onsite. As a part of the analysis, the Final Solar PEIS included a robust suite of design features in the BLM's solar energy program that will be employed to minimize some of the expected impacts of development onsite. The Final Solar PEIS analyzed, and the Solar PEIS ROD adopted, both programmatic and SEZ-specific design features. These design features will be included as stipulations in right-of-way leases for SEZs.

This SRMS addresses the final tier of the mitigation hierarchy, specifically compensatory mitigation, hereafter referred to as regional mitigation. This pilot strategy consists of recommendations to mitigate some of the unavoidable impacts that remain after avoidance and minimization measures are taken. This strategy differs from project-level compensatory mitigation planning that has been conducted in the past. In this pilot, compensatory mitigation is considered in a landscape context and includes identification of mitigation goals and objectives, as well as the selection of mitigation actions based on the degree of impact and regional conditions and trends. This procedure for conducting mitigation is also reflected in the BLM's interim policy, Draft Manual Section 1794, "Regional Mitigation," issued on June 13, 2013.

---

[1] In the Final Solar Energy PEIS (BLM and DOE 2012), Appendix A, Section A.2.5, the BLM refers to solar regional mitigation plans (SRMPs). To be consistent with guidance issued in BLM Instruction Memorandum 2013-142 (BLM 2013b), the BLM adopts the terminology of solar regional mitigation strategies (SRMSs).

1.3 Solar Regional Mitigation Strategy Process

In August 2012, the BLM initiated the pilot Dry Lake SEZ Solar Regional Mitigation Planning Project, which constitutes the first SRMS developed for an SEZ. The Dry Lake SEZ SRMS originated simultaneously with, and served as a pilot test case for, the establishment of BLM guidance for developing SRMSs for other SEZs (BLM forthcoming). The effort was conducted with a significant amount of public involvement, including four workshops, several web-based meetings, and opportunities to comment on preliminary and draft versions of methodologies and strategies.

The Dry Lake SEZ is located about 15 mi (24 km) northeast of Las Vegas in Nevada. The process for developing the Dry Lake SEZ SRMS largely followed the outline for regional mitigation planning outlined in the Final Solar PEIS. In general, a team of specialists from the BLM Southern Nevada District Office, with the support of Argonne National Laboratory, produced a preliminary product at each step in the process, which was then presented and discussed in a public forum. The opportunity for written comments was also extended to the public. The content and methods used in this process incorporate many of the ideas and comments received from the public.

The mitigation actions identified in this strategy are designed to compensate for the loss of some of the habitat, visual resources, and ecological services that are expected from the development of the Dry Lake SEZ. For the purpose of this analysis, it is assumed that all of the developable land within the Dry Lake SEZ will be impacted. The degree of compensation will take into consideration the condition of the resource values present in the Dry Lake SEZ and also consider the relative costs and benefits of the use of public lands for solar energy development, including the amount of time and effort required to restore the disturbed area upon expiration of the lease. The recommended mitigation actions are drawn from the "Proposed Las Vegas Resource Management Plan and Final Environmental Impact Statement" (Las Vegas RMP) (BLM 1998). They consist of restoration and preservation measures prescribed for the Gold Butte Area of Critical Environmental Concern (ACEC), but for which sufficient resources have been unavailable. The Gold Butte ACEC is in the same ecological zone (ecoregion) and subzone as the Dry Lake SEZ and is of the same vegetation community. The Gold Butte ACEC provides habitat for all of the wildlife, including the special status species, found in the Dry Lake SEZ.

Under the terms of this strategy, funding derived from mitigation fees for the Dry Lake SEZ will not be sufficient to fund all of the potential restoration and protection needs in the Gold Butte ACEC, but they will allow significant progress toward achieving the management objectives for the ACEC: to preserve the extraordinary resource values found there while providing for human use and enjoyment. As part of the proposed solar energy program, the solar long-term monitoring program will be used to evaluate the effectiveness of mitigation strategies employed through regional mitigation plans. Regional mitigation strategies will be subject to continued review and adjustment by the BLM and its partners to ensure conservation goals and objectives are being met.

1.4 Stakeholder Involvement in the Solar Regional Mitigation Strategy Process

The pilot process for including stakeholder input in developing the Dry Lake SEZ SRMS included four workshops in Las Vegas and several web-based meetings. Representatives from federal, state, and local government agencies; nongovernmental organizations concerned with issues such as environmental or recreational impacts; representatives from the solar development industry, mining industry, and utilities; tribal representatives; and individual members of the public who had been involved in the Solar PEIS process were invited to attend these activities. Approximately 70 individuals and representatives from the previously mentioned organizations attended the kickoff workshop held August 29-30, 2012. During the first workshop, background on regional mitigation planning and the Solar PEIS impact assessment for the Dry Lake SEZ were provided to the attendees. The subsequent three workshops all had about 35 attendees, including individuals and representatives from agencies, nongovernmental organizations, the solar industry and consultants to the industry, utilities, and tribes.

The second workshop was held October 24-25, 2012. This workshop included a field visit to the Dry Lake SEZ in order to give the participants a firsthand look at the SEZ. BLM staff experts were present and spoke about the range of resources present in the SEZ and possible opportunities available to avoid, minimize, and mitigate potential impacts related to solar energy development.

The third workshop was held January 30-31, 2013. This workshop focused on regional trends and conditions, unavoidable impacts that may warrant regional mitigation, the establishment of regional mitigation objectives, the use of mapping tools and data in choosing locations for mitigation, prioritization of mitigation projects, mitigation costing, and long-term monitoring.

The fourth workshop, held on February 27, 2013, focused on three topics: (1) methods for establishing mitigation fees in SEZs, and specifically in the Dry Lake SEZ; (2) establishing solar mitigation objectives and priority setting; and (3) structures for holding and applying mitigation funds.

Additionally, several webinars were held to provide information on: mitigation valuation methods and mitigation structure options (December 6, 2012); methods to identify impacts that may warrant mitigation (January 1, 2013); and a proposed mitigation fee setting method and method to evaluate candidate mitigation sites (March 21, 2013).

All presentations from the four workshops and three webinars are posted on the project documents web page on the Dry Lake SEZ SRMS Project website at: http://www.blm.gov/nv/st/en/fo/lvfo/blm_programs/energy/dry_lake_solar_energy.html. Reports from the workshops are also available. Additional materials that were provided for stakeholder review are posted on the project website documents page as well.

Throughout the pilot project, stakeholders were invited to comment on interim draft materials, including the summary of unavoidable impacts at the Dry Lake SEZ that may warrant mitigation, the proposed method for deriving the mitigation fees, the method of evaluating candidate sites for mitigation, and the specific mitigation sites and activities proposed for the Dry Lake SEZ. Many of these comments were discussed during workshops and used to guide development of this strategy.

2.1 Description of the Dry Lake Solar Energy Zone and Surrounding Region

2.1.1 General Description of the Solar Energy Zone

The Dry Lake SEZ is located in Clark County in southern Nevada. The total area of the Dry Lake SEZ, as shown in Figure 2-1, is 6,187 acres (25 km²) (BLM and DOE 2012). In the Final Solar PEIS and the Solar PEIS ROD, 469 acres (1.9 km²) of floodplain and wetland within the SEZ boundaries were identified as nondevelopment areas. The developable area of the SEZ given in the Final Solar PEIS was 5,717 acres (23 km²).

The towns of Moapa and Overton are located 18 mi (29 km) northeast and 23 mi (37 km) east of the SEZ, respectively. Nellis Air Force Base is located approximately 13 mi (21 km) southwest of the SEZ. The nearest major roads accessing the proposed Dry Lake SEZ are Interstate 15, which passes along the southeastern boundary of the SEZ, and U.S. Route 93, which runs from north to south along part of the southwest border of the SEZ. The Union Pacific Railroad runs north to south along a portion of the eastern SEZ boundary, with the nearest stop in Las Vegas. The area around the SEZ is not highly populated, although Clark County, with a 2008 population close to 2 million individuals, has a large number of residents.

The SEZ already contains rights-of-way and developed areas, including energy, water, and transportation infrastructure

facilities. Three designated transmission corridors pass through the area, including a Section 368 energy corridor (of the Energy Policy Act of 2005), which contains numerous electric transmission lines, natural gas and refined petroleum product lines, and water lines (see Figure 2-1 for the designated corridor). A power generating station is also located within the area of the SEZ, and two existing natural gas power plants are located just southwest of the SEZ on private land. A minerals processing plant is located in the southeastern corner of the SEZ. The Final Solar PEIS indicated that in 2012 there were three pending solar applications within or adjacent to the SEZ and an additional large application area located about 2 mi (3 km) to the east of the SEZ across Interstate 15.

2.1.2 Landscape Conditions of the Solar Energy Zone and the Region

In 2012, the BLM completed the "Mojave Basin and Range Rapid Ecoregional Assessment" for the Mojave Basin and Range ecoregion in which the Dry Lake SEZ is located (NatureServe 2013). The Mojave Basin and Range REA examines broad-scale ecological values, conditions, and trends within the ecoregion by synthesizing existing

spatial datasets in a meaningful timeframe. The REAs serve multiple purposes in an ecoregional context, including identifying and answering important management questions; understanding key resource values; understanding the influence of various change agents; understanding projected ecological trends; identifying and mapping key opportunities for resource conservation, restoration, and development; and providing a baseline to evaluate and guide future actions.

One useful product of the REAs is the development of landscape condition models. These geospatial models have been created to represent the condition or level of intactness throughout the ecoregion at the time in which the assessments were initiated (approximately 2010). The landscape condition model is a combination of two primary factors—land use and a distance decay function from land uses. Different land use categories were assigned a relative value between 0 and 1, representing very high landscape alteration to very little landscape alteration. For example, high-density urban areas received values closer to 0, whereas intact undisturbed areas received values closer to 1. The distance decay function considered the proximity of each location to human land uses. Table 2-1 lists a number of examples of land use and distance decay scores for various stressor categories in the Mojave Basin and

Range. A full description of the landscape condition model and how it was developed can be found in the "Mojave Basin and Range Rapid Ecoregional Assessments Final Memorandum I-3-C."

The landscape condition model developed for the Mojave Basin and Range was developed as a raster dataset of 100-m cells.

The model illustrates landscape condition values throughout the ecoregion (Figure 2-2). The resulting map provides a composite view of the relative impacts of land uses across the entire ecoregion. Darker green areas indicate apparently least impacted areas (most intact) and orange-red areas are the most impacted (least intact). According

to this landscape condition model, most of the impacts occur near urban areas (e.g., Las Vegas) and along roadways. However, most of the Mojave Basin and Range is still relatively intact. The landscape condition within the Dry Lake SEZ is shown in Figure 2-3.

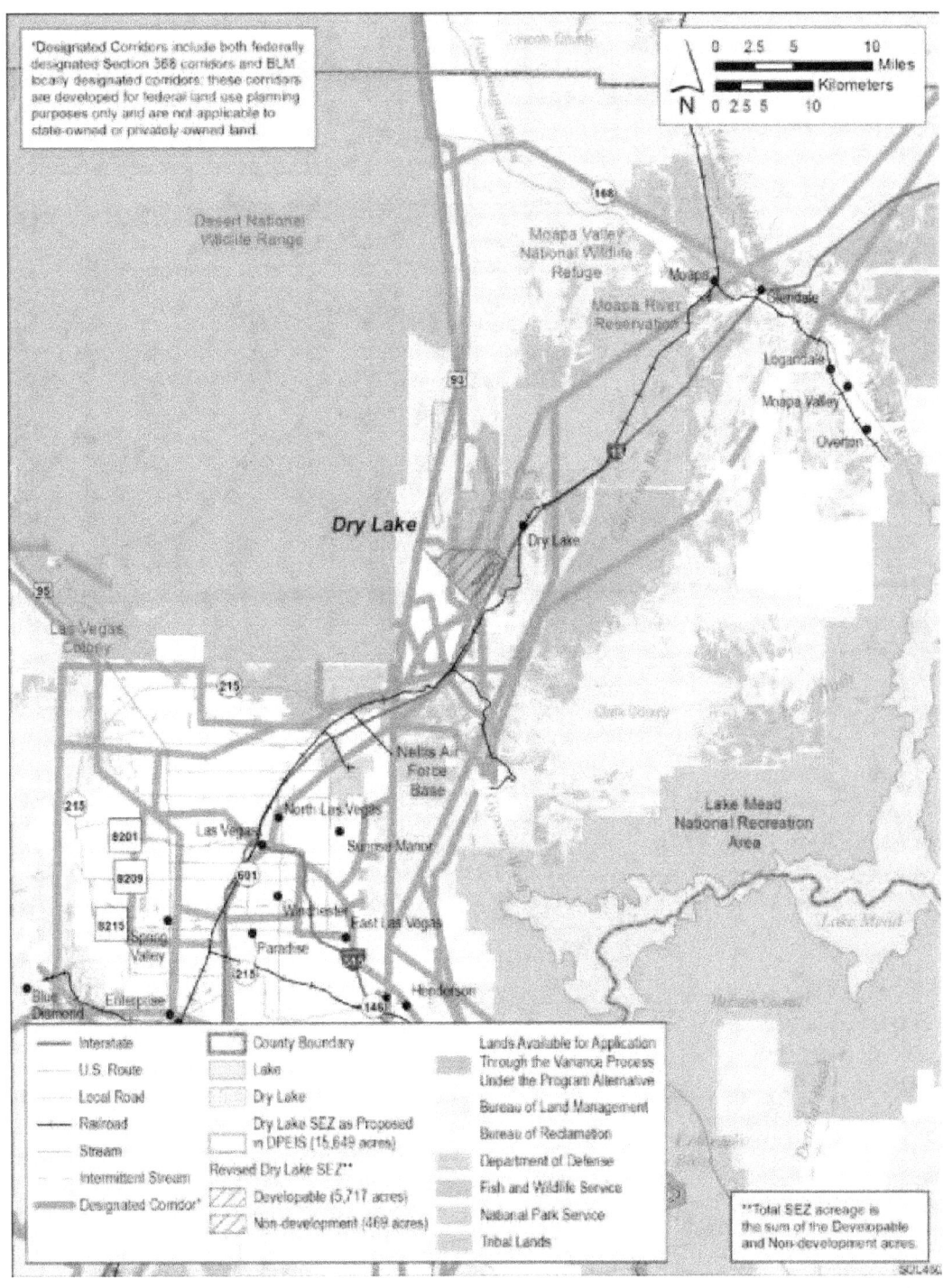

Figure 2-1. Dry Lake Solar Energy Zone and surrounding area (Source: BLM and DOE 2012).

2.1.3 Regional Setting

2.1.3.1 General Description

The Dry Lake SEZ is situated within 5 mi (8 km) of several other federally owned or administered lands. The Moapa River Indian Reservation is approximately 4 mi (6.4 km) northeast of the revised SEZ boundary. The Coyote Springs ACEC, which is also designated critical habitat for the federally threatened desert tortoise, is located within 0.5 mi (0.8 km) west of the SEZ. Farther west of the Coyote Springs ACEC is the U.S. Fish and Wildlife Service Desert National Wildlife Refuge, which is approximately 3 mi (4.8 km) west of the SEZ. The Muddy Mountains Wilderness Area is approximately 8 mi (12.9 km) southeast of the SEZ (Figure 2-4).

The Dry Lake SEZ is located in a relatively undeveloped rural area, bounded on the west by the Arrow Canyon Range and on the southeast by the Dry Lake Range. The topography of the land within the SEZ is arid basin dominated by creosote and white bursage vegetation communities. Land cover types[2] within the ecoregion are presented in Figure 2-5. At a more local scale, land cover types in the vicinity of the Dry Lake SEZ are shown in Figure 2-6. In total, there are 10 natural land cover types and 2 disturbance land cover types predicted to occur in the vicinity (i.e., within 5 mi, or 8 km) of the Dry Lake SEZ (Table 2-2). There are three land cover types that occur in the developable portion of the SEZ (Table 2-2). Listed in order of dominance, these land cover types are: Sonora-Mojave Creosote-White Bursage Desert Scrub (98.8% of the developable area), Sonora-Mojave

Mixed Salt Desert Scrub (0.8% of the developable area), and North American Warm Desert Wash (0.4% of the developable area). Other land cover types expected to occur in the nondevelopable area of the SEZ include Developed, Medium – High Intensity and North American Warm Desert Pavement (Table 2-2).

Table 2-1. Ecological stressor source, site-impact scores, and distance decay scores implemented for the landscape condition model for the Mojave Basin and Range.

Ecological Stressor Source	Site Impact Score	Presumed Relative Stress	Distance Decay Score	Impact Approaches Negligible
Transportation				
Dirt roads, 4-wheel drive	0.7	Low	0.5	200 m
Local, neighborhood and connecting roads	0.5	Medium	0.5	200 m
Secondary and connecting roads	0.2	High	0.2	500 m
Primary highways with limited access	0.05	Very High	0.1	1,000 m
Primary highways without limited access	0.05	Very High	0.05	2,000 m
Urban and Industrial Development				
Low-density development	0.6	Medium	0.5	200 m
Medium-density development	0.5	Medium	0.5	200 m
Powerline/transmission lines	0.5	Medium	0.9	100 m
Oil/gas wells	0.5	Medium	0.2	500 m
High-density development	0.05	Very High	0.05	2,000 m
Mines	0.05	Very High	0.2	500 m
Managed and Modified Land Cover				
Ruderal forest and upland	0.9	Very Low	1	0 m
Native vegetation with introduced species	0.9	Very Low	1	0 m
Pasture	0.9	Very Low	0.9	100 m
Recently logged	0.9	Very Low	0.5	200 m
Managed tree plantations	0.8	Low	0.5	200 m
Introduced tree and shrub	0.5	Medium	0.5	200 m
Introduced upland grass and forb	0.5	Medium	0.5	200 m
Introduced wetland	0.3	High	0.8	125 m
Cultivated agriculture	0.3	High	0.5	200 m

2.1.3.2 Problematic Regional Trends

The Mojave Basin and Range REA presents a framework for determining the condition and trend of various resource values and conservation elements in the ecoregion. The Mojave Basin and Range REA defines conservation elements as resources of conservation concern within an ecoregion. These elements could include habitat or populations for plant and animal taxa, such as threatened and endangered species, or ecological systems and

---

[2] Geospatial data for land cover types were obtained from the Southwest Regional Gap Analysis Project (http://earth.gis.usu.edu/swgap/) and the California Gap land cover mapping project (http://gap.uidaho.edu/index.php/california-land-cover/).

plant communities of regional importance. A list of conservation elements could also include other resource values, such as highly erodible soils; populations of wild horses and burros; scenic viewsheds; or designated sites of natural, historical, or cultural significance. There are two basic types of conservation elements in the Mojave Basin and Range:

- Coarse filter conservation elements, which typically include all of the major ecosystem types within the assessment landscape and represent all of the predominant natural ecosystem

functions and services in the ecoregion.

- Fine filter conservation elements, which complement the first set of elements by including a limited subset of focal species assemblages and individual species.

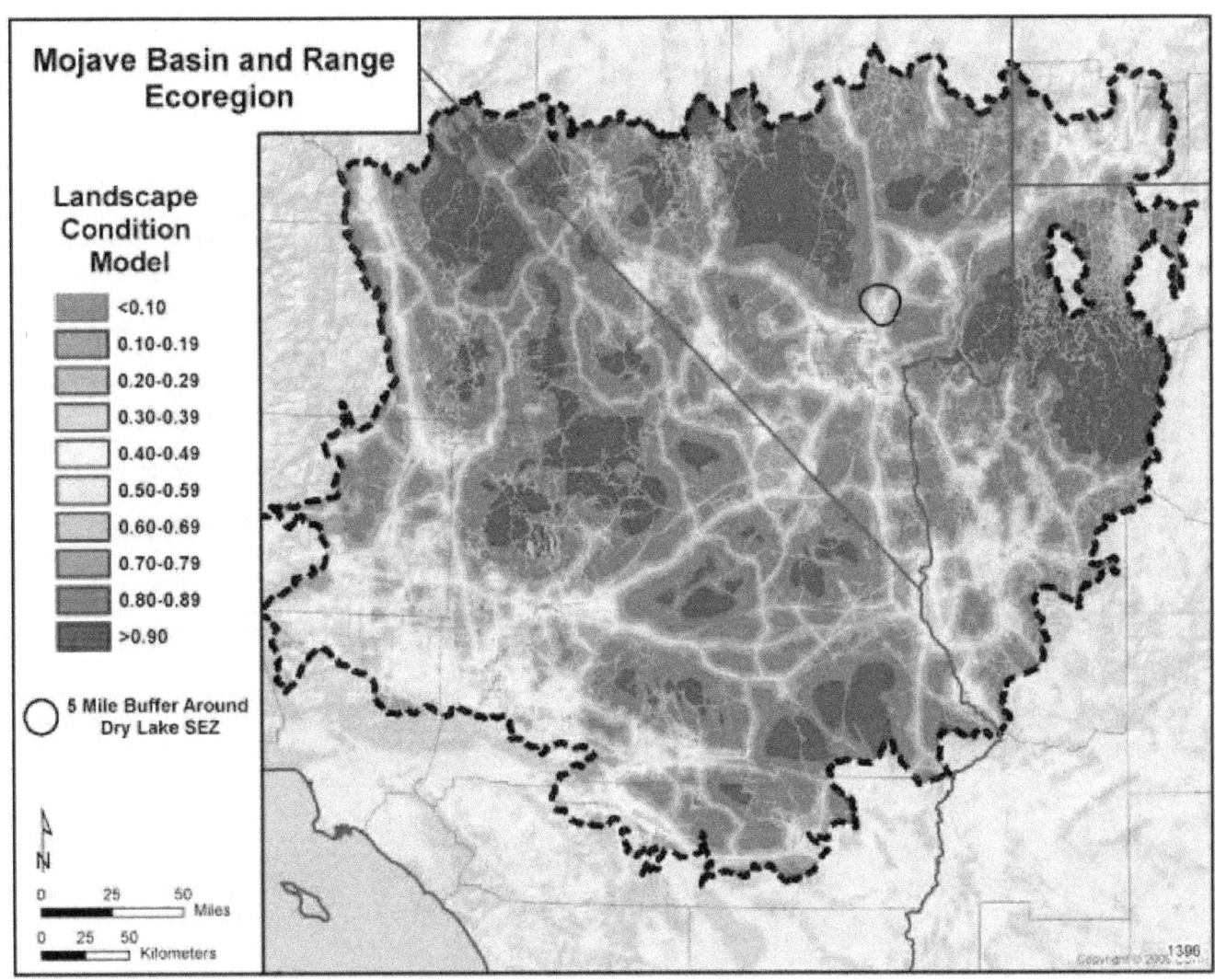

Figure 2-2. Landscape condition in the Mojave Basin and Range ecoregion. Darker green areas indicate least impacted areas (most intact), whereas orange-red areas are the most impacted (least intact). Also shown is the 5-mile buffer around the Dry Lake Solar Energy Zone.

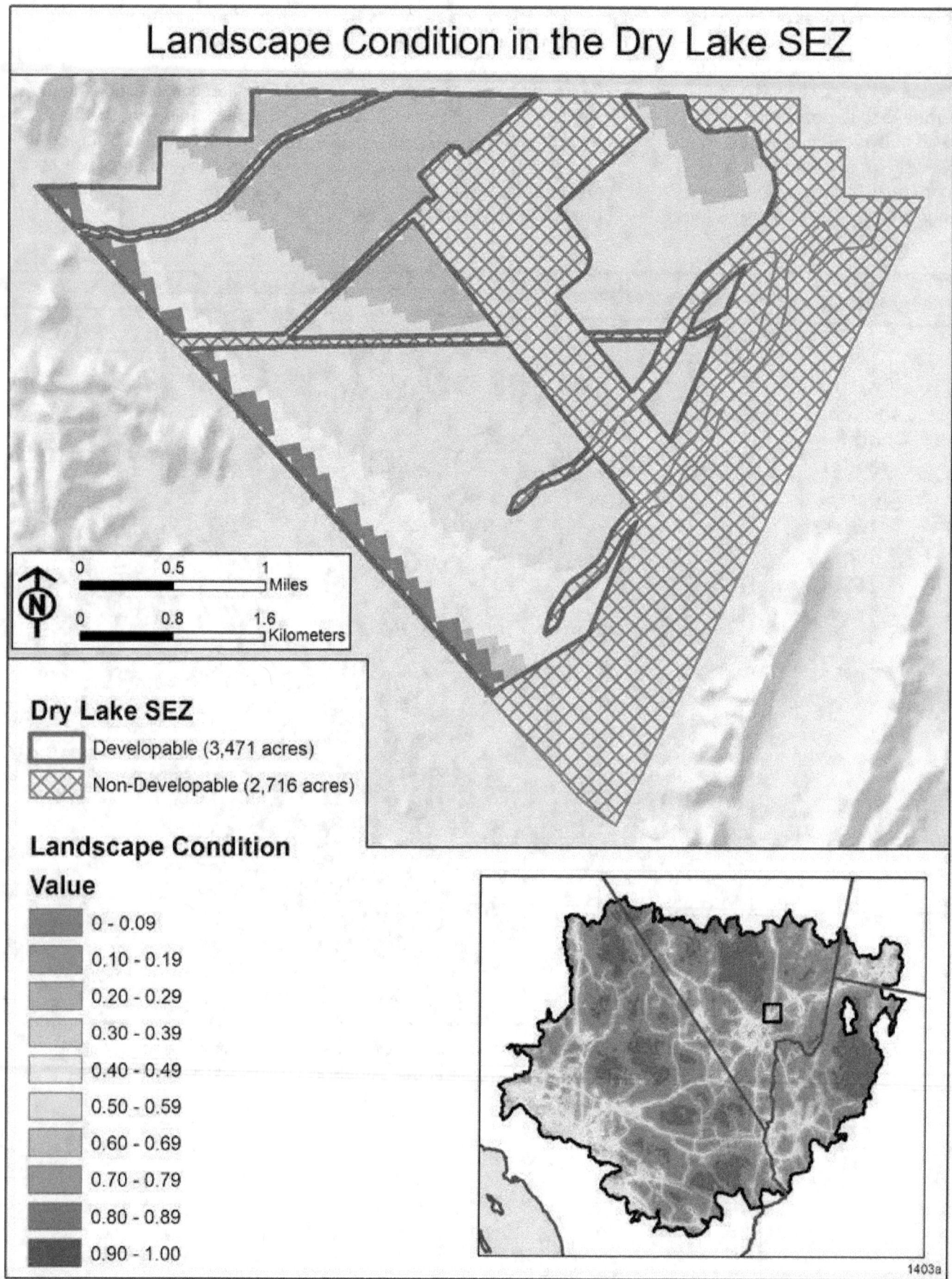

Figure 2-3. Landscape condition in the Dry Lake Solar Energy Zone. Approximately 3,471 acres of the solar energy zone are considered eligible for utility-scale solar energy development.

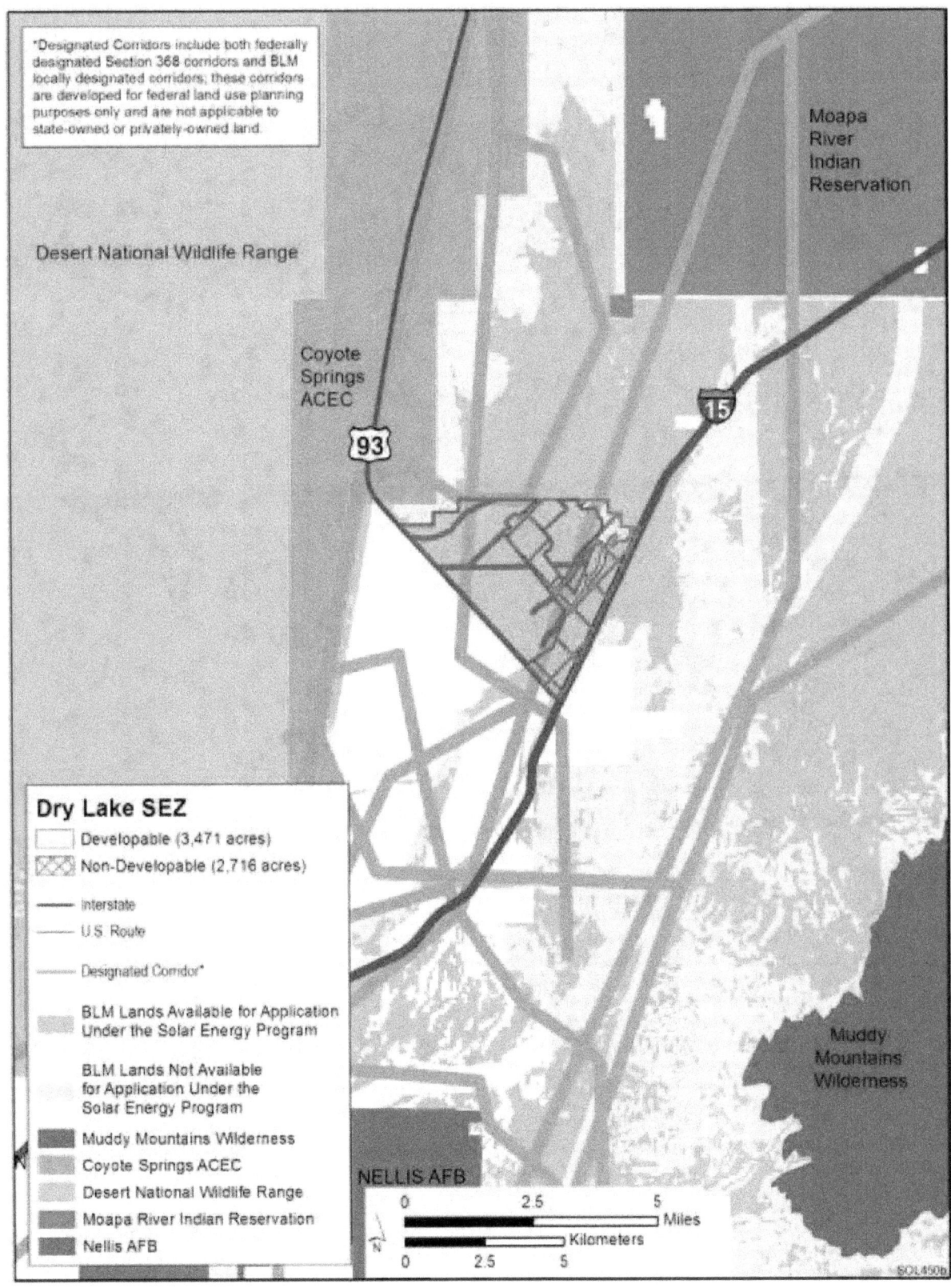

Figure 2-4. Dry Lake Solar Energy Zone and surrounding land designations.

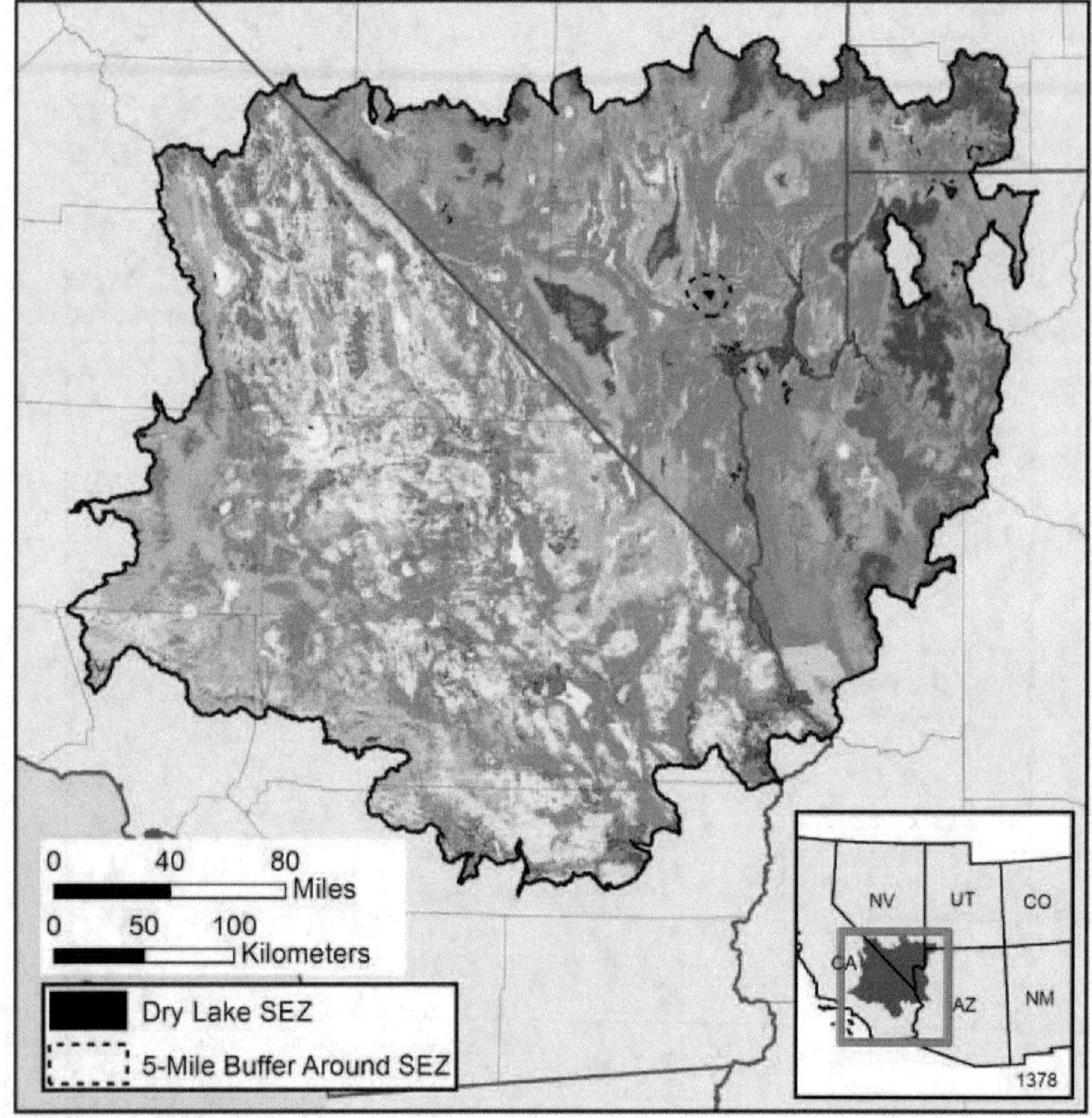

Figure 2-5. Land cover types in the Mojave Basin and Range ecoregion.

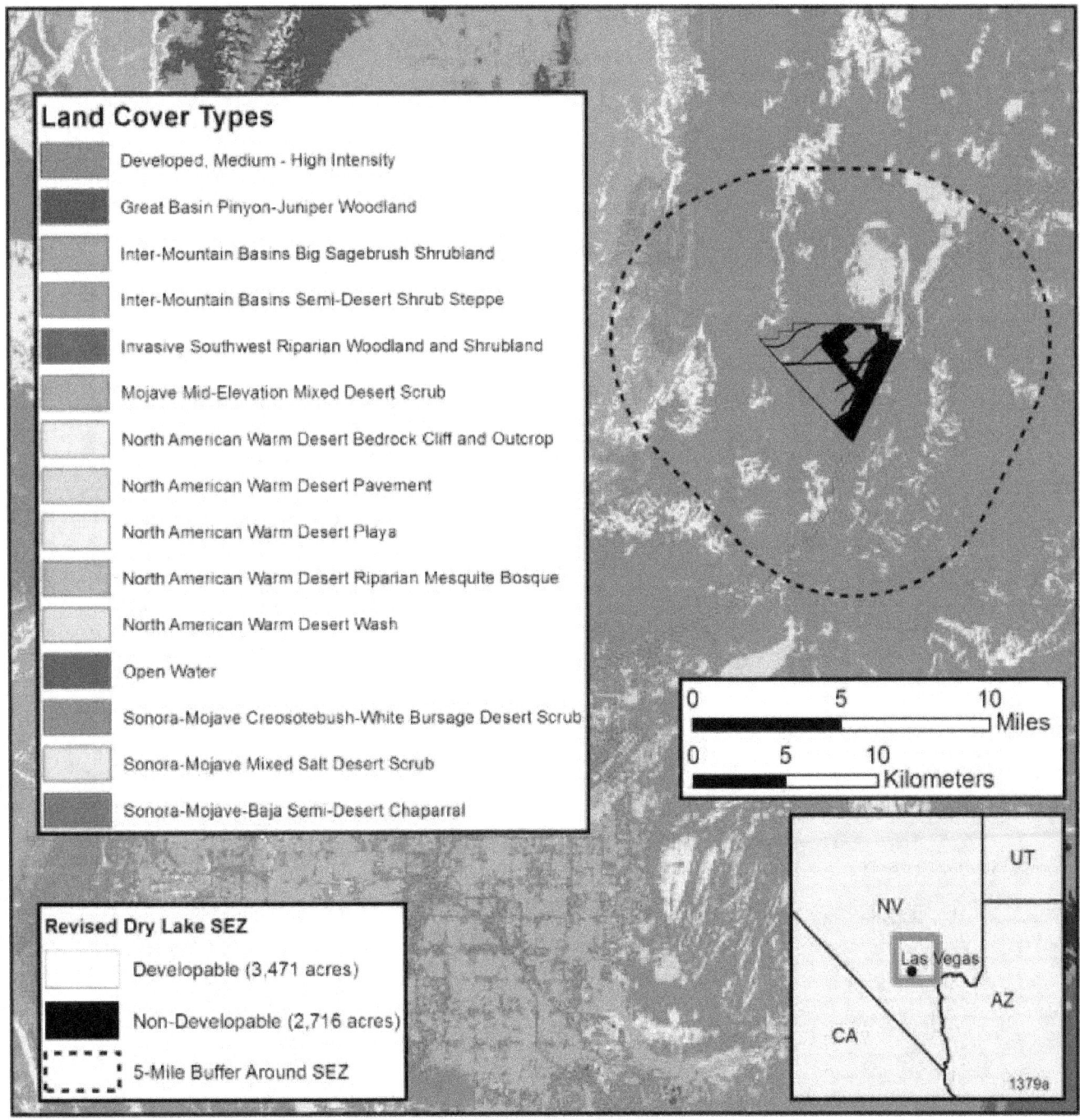

Land Cover Types

- Developed, Medium - High Intensity
- Great Basin Pinyon-Juniper Woodland
- Inter-Mountain Basins Big Sagebrush Shrubland
- Inter-Mountain Basins Semi-Desert Shrub Steppe
- Invasive Southwest Riparian Woodland and Shrubland
- Mojave Mid-Elevation Mixed Desert Scrub
- North American Warm Desert Bedrock Cliff and Outcrop
- North American Warm Desert Pavement
- North American Warm Desert Playa
- North American Warm Desert Riparian Mesquite Bosque
- North American Warm Desert Wash
- Open Water
- Sonora-Mojave Creosotebush-White Bursage Desert Scrub
- Sonora-Mojave Mixed Salt Desert Scrub
- Sonora-Mojave-Baja Semi-Desert Chaparral

Revised Dry Lake SEZ

- Developable (3,471 acres)
- Non-Developable (2,716 acres)
- 5-Mile Buffer Around SEZ

Figure 2-6. Land cover types in the vicinity of the Dry Lake Solar Energy Zone.

Table 2-2. Land cover types and amounts in the vicinity of the Dry Lake Solar Energy Zone.

Description	Acres Within SEZ Developable Area[1]	Acres Within Entire SEZ (Developable and Nondevelopable)[2]	Acres Within 5-Mile Buffer Around SEZ[3]
Natural Land Cover Types			
Sonora-Mojave Creosotebush-White Bursage Desert Scrub	3,427 (98.8%)	5,879 (95.0%)	83,300 (84.1%)
Sonora-Mojave Mixed Salt Desert Scrub	30 (0.8%)	38 (0.6%)	645 (0.7%)
North American Warm Desert Wash	14 (0.4%)	141 (2.3%)	2,618 (2.6%)
North American Warm Desert Pavement		21 (0.3%)	1,694 (1.7%)
North American Warm Desert Bedrock Cliff and Outcrop			5,144 (5.2%)
Mojave Mid-Elevation Mixed Desert Scrub			4,651 (4.7%)
North American Warm Desert Playa			287 (0.3%)
Inter-Mountain Basins Semi-Desert Shrub Steppe			147 (0.1%)
Open Water			1 (<0.1%)
North American Warm Desert Riparian Mesquite Bosque			1 (<0.1%)
Disturbance Land Cover Types			
Developed, Medium - High Intensity		108 (1.8%)	495 (0.5%)
Invasive Southwest Riparian Woodland and Shrubland			11 (<0.1%)
TOTAL (acres):	3,471	6,187	98,994

[1] Values in parentheses represent the percent acreage relative to the entire developable area (3,471 acres).

[2] Values in parentheses represent the percent acreage relative to the entire SEZ (6,187 acres).

[3] Values in parentheses represent the percent acreage relative to the entire 5-mile buffer area (98,994 acres).

A full list and explanation of the coarse filter conservation elements within the Mojave Basin and Range can be found in Appendix 2 of the Mojave Basin and Range REA. In brief, the core conservation elements include 19 coarse filter conservation elements that represent terrestrial and aquatic ecological system types and communities and more than 600 fine filter conservation elements that represent individual species or species assemblages.

Problematic trends are understood by forecasting the response of conservation elements to one of four change agents in the ecoregion. The four change agents include fire, invasive species, climate change, and human development. Of these change agents, the conservation element responses to human development are the easiest to predict in a meaningful timeframe for SRMSs because solar energy development represents an anthropogenic disturbance, and the impacts of human development are likely to affect all conservation elements similarly.

Understanding the problematic conservation element trends relevant to the Dry Lake SEZ was accomplished through (1) a geospatial analysis of available ecoregional data and (2) expert opinion by the BLM interdisciplinary team. Figure 2-7 presents a conceptual illustration of the geospatial framework for determining the condition and trends of conservation elements in the ecoregion. The geospatial data used in this assessment are available publicly from open sources. These data include the BLM's landscape condition model for the Mojave Basin and Range, modeled land cover types, and species-specific habitat suitability models. The Mojave Basin and Range landscape condition model can be used as a proxy for landscape intactness. Evaluating condition and trends of coarse and fine filter conservation elements (land cover and habitat models) in an ecoregional context will provide a better understanding of the impacts of solar energy development within the Dry Lake SEZ relative to the rest of the ecoregion.

The geospatial process for quantitatively evaluating condition and trends for conservation elements (Figure 2-7) begins with a characterization of the distribution of the conservation element within identified analysis areas: (1) the entire Mojave Basin and Range ecoregion, (2) vicinity of the Dry Lake SEZ, and (3) within the Dry Lake SEZ developable area. These areas are then clipped to current and anticipated future

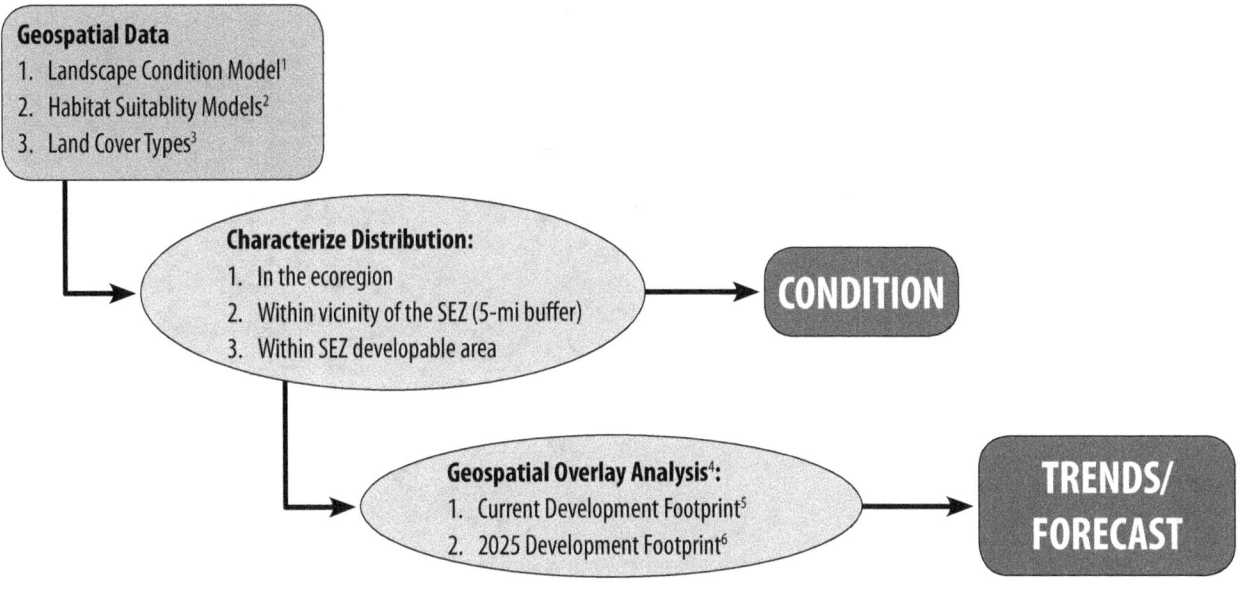

[1] The landscape condition model is available from and described in the BLM Mojave Basin and Range Rapid Ecoregional Assessment.

[2] Habitat suitability models are available from the Southwest Regional Gap Analysis Project.

[3] Land cover types are available from the Southwest Regional Gap Analysis Project.

[4] The overlay change agent/conservation element analysis was conducted to determine geospatial trends. Geospatial data for the change agent were overlayed with the distribution of conservation elements to determine current and future distributions of the conservation elements.

[5] Geospatial data for the current human development footprint model are available from and described in the BLM Mojave Basin and Range Rapid Ecoregional Assessment.

[6] Geospatial data for the future (approximately 2025) human development footprint model are available from and described in the BLM Mojave Basin and Range Rapid Ecoregional Assessment.

Figure 2-7. Conceptual diagram for estimating condition and trends of conservation elements in the Mojave Basin and Range ecoregion for the Dry Lake Solar Energy Zone Solar Regional Mitigation Strategy.

human development footprints[3] and forecast trends. Trends are understood by using the current and future human development footprints to evaluate the expected future distribution of the conservation element relative to its current distribution.

An example table showing the condition and trends of various coarse and fine filter conservation elements in the Mojave Basin and Range is shown in Table 2-3. Due to the large number of fine scale conservation elements that could potentially be evaluated, the BLM determined that a trends analysis of coarse filter land cover types would be a suitable habitat-based proxy

for geospatial trends of fine scale conservation elements (individual species). In Table 2-3, coarse filter conservation elements evaluated include the Mojave Basin and Range landscape condition model and the Southwest Regional Gap Analysis Project modeled land cover types.

The only fine filter conservation element presented in Table 2-3 is the Mojave population of the desert tortoise (*Gopherus agassizii*), which is listed in the table due to its threatened status under the Endangered Species Act and known presence in potentially suitable habitat on the Dry Lake SEZ. Based on the results presented in Table 2-3, it was concluded that all conservation elements are

expected to experience a declining trend in the Mojave Basin and Range, as all conservation elements are expected to experience some level of range contraction due to human development in the future. Landscape condition within the Mojave Basin and Range is also expected to decline in the future. Because the Sonora-Mojave Creosotebush-White Bursage Desert Scrub comprised the largest portion of the Dry Lake SEZ (98.8%), the cumulative expected future loss of this conservation element of 10.26% was considered to be a problematic trend among all conservation elements relative to the Dry Lake SEZ.

[3] Geospatial data for current and future human development footprints are described in more detail in the Mojave Basin and Range REA (NatureServe 2013).

Table 2-3. Condition and trends assessment for coarse and fine filter conservation elements in the Mojave Basin and Range relevant to the Dry Lake Solar Energy Zone.

Description	Solar Energy Zone (SEZ) Site-Specific Condition (SEZ Developable Area)		Condition in the Vicinity of SEZ (Local-Regional Status)		Landscape-Ecoregional Condition		Ecoregional Trends[a]			
	Potential Distribution (Acres) Within SEZ	Percent Within SEZ Relative to Distribution in Ecoregion	Potential Distribution (Acres) Within 5 mi of SEZ Boundary	Percent Within 5 mi Area Relative to Distribution in Ecoregion	Potential Distribution (Acres) Within Mojave Ecoregion	Percent Total Distribution Within Ecoregion	Current Conversion to Human Development (Acres)	Percent Current Conversion Relative to Distribution in Ecoregion	Future Conversion to Human Development (Acres)	Percent Future Conversion Relative to Distribution in Ecoregion
Natural Land Cover Types										
Sonora-Mojave Creosotebush-White Bursage Desert Scrub	3,428	0.02%	83,300	0.59%	14,085,230	34.73%	1,229,275	8.73%	1,444,510	10.26%
North American Warm Desert Wash	14	<0.01%	2,618	0.45%	585,954	1.44%	36,307	6.20%	49,560	8.46%
Sonora-Mojave Mixed Salt Desert Scrub	29	<0.01%	645	0.04%	1,486,560	3.66%	370,165	24.90%	401,792	27.03%
North American Warm Desert Pavement			1,694	0.30%	570,572	1.41%	21,738	3.81%	22,730	3.98%
North American Warm Desert Bedrock Cliff and Outcrop			5,144	0.08%	6,082,940	15.00%	159,812	2.63%	177,422	2.92%
Mojave Mid-Elevation Mixed Desert Scrub			4,651	0.07%	6,263,875	15.44%	403,753	6.45%	447,348	7.14%
North American Warm Desert Playa			287	0.04%	723,597	1.78%	34,661	4.79%	37,391	5.17%
Inter-Mountain Basins Semi-Desert Shrub Steppe			147	0.02%	866,500	2.14%	29,719	3.43%	37,847	4.37%
Open Water			1	0.00%	234,039	0.58%	4,439	1.90%	5,861	2.50%
North American Warm Desert Riparian Mesquite Bosque			1	0.01%	17,732	0.04%	3,316	18.70%	3,499	19.74%
Great Basin Pinyon-Juniper Woodland					2,085,200	5.14%	63,364	3.04%	69,027	3.31%
Sonora-Mojave-Baja Semi-Desert Chaparral					24,559	0.06%	1,120	4.56%	1,192	4.86%
Inter-Mountain Basins Big Sagebrush Shrubland					701,289	1.73%	20,766	2.96%	21,571	3.08%
Disturbance Land Cover Types										
Developed, Medium – High Intensity			495	0.39%	128,405	0.32%	115,830	90.21%	118,686	92.43%
Invasive Southwest Riparian Woodland and Shrubland			11	0.02%	52,262	0.13%	20,726	39.66%	24,288	46.47%
TOTAL	3,471	<0.01%	98,994	2.91%	33,908,714	83.60%	2,514,991	7.42%	2,862,724	8.44%

[a] The trend assessment included the current and future (approximately 2025) development footprints to determine the amount of each land cover type that is expected to be converted to human developments.

Table 2-3 (continued).

	Solar Energy Zone (SEZ) Site-Specific Condition (SEZ Developable Area)	Condition in the Vicinity of SEZ (Local-Regional Status)	Landscape-Ecoregional Condition	Ecoregional Trends[a]	
Coarse Filter Conservation Element: Landscape Condition Model					
	Average Current Condition Value Within the SEZ (SD*)	**Average Current Condition Value Within 5 mi of SEZ Boundary (SD*)**	**Average Current Condition Value Within Mojave Basin and Range Ecoregion (SD*)**	**Average Future Condition Value Within Mojave Basin and Range Ecoregion (SD*)**	**Average Ecoregional Difference in Current and Future Condition Values (%)**
Landscape Condition Value	57.4 (5.0)	66.0 (9.4)	76.6 (13.8)	72.3 (17.3)	-4.3 (5.6%)
Fine Filter Conservation Element: Mojave Desert Tortoise Distribution					
	Potential Distribution (Acres) Within SEZ	**Potential Distribution (Acres) Within 5 mi of SEZ Boundary**	**Potential Distribution (Acres) Within Mojave Ecoregion**	**Future Conversion to Human Development (Acres)**	**Percent Future Conversion**
Mojave Desert Tortoise Potentially Suitable Habitat Model (SWReGAP)	3,471	92,168	16,772,653	1,059,811	6.3%
*SD = standard deviation					

2.2 General Description of Solar Development in the Dry Lake Solar Energy Zone

2.2.1 Description of Existing Rights-of-Way and Impact on Developable Area

As stated in Section 2.1, the Dry Lake SEZ contains many previously developed areas, including a natural gas power plant (the Harry Allen Generating Station), pipelines, a gypsum mining processing plant, several known mining claims, and three designated transmission corridors and rights-of-way (including a 500-kilovolt transmission line) (Figure 2-4).

Subsequent to the signing of the Solar PEIS ROD, BLM Southern Nevada District Office staff revised the developable and nondevelopable portions of the SEZ to take into account current existing land uses on the SEZ. Known locations of rights-of-way, pipelines, and existing leases and mining claims, including the natural gas power plant and gypsum processing plant, have been identified as nondevelopment areas within the SEZ. Although the total SEZ size is the same as that reported in the Final Solar PEIS (6,187 acres, or 25 km²), the developable area of the SEZ has been reduced from 5,717 acres (23 km²) to 3,471 acres (14 km²) (Figure 2-8).

2.2.2 Description of Potential Development

Utility-scale solar facilities of all technology types have a key element in common—they all have a large solar field with reflectors or photovoltaic surfaces designed to capture the sun's energy. The solar fields generally require a relatively flat land surface; only locations with less than 5% slope were included as SEZs in the Final Solar PEIS. As constructed to date, vegetation is generally cleared and solar fields are fenced to prevent damage to or from wildlife and trespassers.

In the Final Solar PEIS, maximum solar development of the Dry Lake SEZ was assumed to be 80% of the developable SEZ area over a period of 20 years. Although the developable area has been refined to 3,471 acres (14 km²) (see Section 2.2.1), for the purposes of this assessment, it is assumed that more nondevelopment areas will be identified in the future and that only approximately 3,000 acres (12 km²) will be developed (see Section 2.5). In the Final Solar PEIS, data from various existing solar facilities were used to estimate that solar trough facilities will require about 5 acres/megawatt (0.02 km²/megawatt), and other types of solar facilities (e.g., power tower, dish engine, and photovoltaic technologies) will require about 9 acres/megawatt (0.04 km²/megawatt). Using these land requirement assumptions, full development of the Dry Lake SEZ, assuming the revised developable area, would allow development of solar facilities with an estimated total of between 386 megawatts (for power tower, dish engine, or photovoltaic technologies) and 694 megawatts (for solar trough technologies) of electrical power capacity.

Availability of transmission from SEZs to load centers is an important consideration for future development in SEZs. For the proposed Dry Lake SEZ, several existing transmission lines, including a 500-kilovolt line, run through the SEZ. It is possible that an existing line could be used to provide access from the SEZ to the transmission grid, but since existing lines may already be at full capacity, it is possible that at full build-out capacity, new transmission and/or upgrades of existing transmission lines may be required to bring electricity from the proposed Dry Lake SEZ to load centers. An assessment of the most likely load center destinations for power generated at the Dry Lake SEZ and a general assessment of the impacts of constructing and operating new transmission facilities on those load centers was provided in Section 11.3.23 of the Final Solar PEIS. Project-specific analyses would also be required to identify the specific impacts of new transmission construction and line upgrades for any projects proposed within the SEZ.

Since Interstate 15 and U.S. Route 93 are adjacent to the SEZ, existing road access should be adequate to support construction and operation of solar facilities. It is likely that no additional road construction outside of the SEZ would be needed.

2.3 Summary of Solar Development Impacts on the Dry Lake Solar Energy Zone

A comprehensive assessment of the potential impacts of solar development at the Dry Lake SEZ was provided in the Final Solar PEIS (BLM and DOE 2012). Potential adverse impacts included effects on nearby wilderness areas, recreational use of the SEZ lands, military use of the SEZ lands, soils, water resources, vegetation, wildlife, special status species (both vegetation and wildlife), air quality, visual resources, paleontological and cultural resources, Native American concerns, and transportation.

Some potential positive impacts of development were identified for local socioeconomics, as well as positive impacts in terms of potential to reduce greenhouse gas emissions if solar energy produced at the SEZ would displace use of fossil fuels.

2.4 Mitigation Strategy (Hierarchy) of the Dry Lake Solar Energy Zone

2.4.1 Avoidance

2.4.1.1 Dry Wash/Riparian Areas

In the Final Solar PEIS and the Solar PEIS ROD, 469 acres (1.9 km²) of floodplain and wetland within the SEZ boundaries were identified as nondevelopment areas. Avoidance of these areas will eliminate or largely reduce adverse impacts to them.

2.4.1.2 Existing Rights-of-Way, Mining Claims, etc.

As stated in Section 2.2.1, the BLM has revised the developable and nondevelopable portions of the SEZ to take into account current existing land uses on the SEZ. Known locations of rights-of-way, pipelines, and existing leases and mining claims, including the natural gas power plant and gypsum processing plant, have been identified as nondevelopment areas within the SEZ. The remaining developable area of the SEZ has been reduced to 3,471 acres (14 km²) (Figure 2-8). This reduction in developable area of the SEZ also will reduce potential impacts identified in the Final Solar PEIS (e.g., far fewer acres of habitat reduction will occur for vegetation and wildlife species, including special status species). In addition, an eligible archaeological site (i.e., Old Spanish Trail/Mormon Road) within a right-of-way will be avoided.

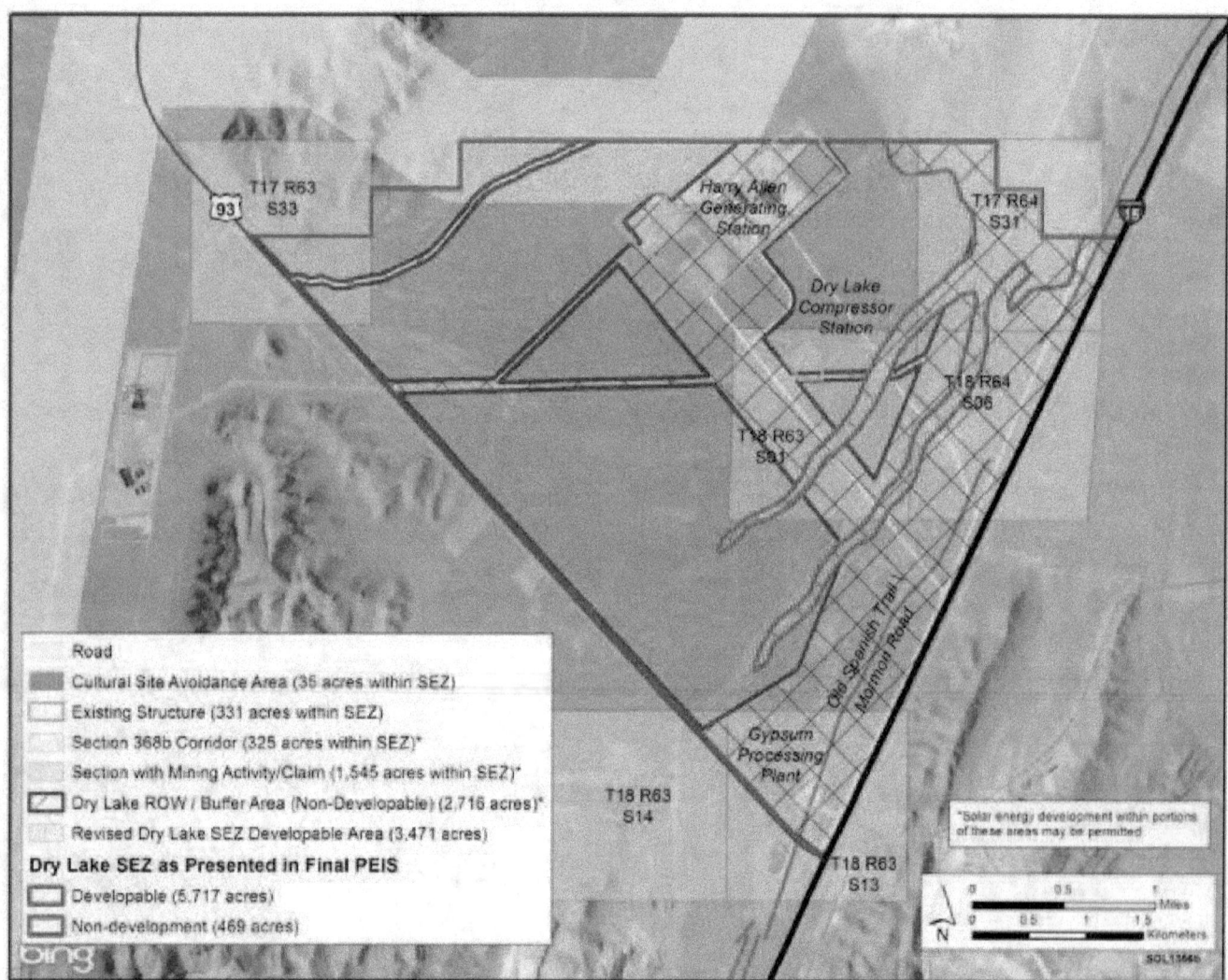

Figure 2-8. Dry Lake Solar Energy Zone revised developable area.

2.4.2 Minimization

2.4.2.1 Summary of Programmatic Design Features to be Applied

The Final Solar PEIS identified a comprehensive suite of required programmatic design features that would avoid and/or minimize adverse impacts to resources, either onsite or through consultation/coordination with potentially affected entities. The programmatic design features are extensive and are listed in their entirety in Appendix A of the Solar PEIS ROD (BLM 2012). These programmatic design features include required actions to avoid or minimize impacts to all of the potentially impacted resources listed in Section 2.3.

2.4.2.2 Other Required Impact Minimization Measures and/or Stipulations

The Final Solar PEIS also includes SEZ-specific design features for all of the SEZs. The SEZ-specific design features identified for the Dry Lake SEZ were the following:

Water resources: Groundwater analyses suggest that full build-out of dry-cooled and wet-cooled technologies is not feasible; for mixed-technology development scenarios, any proposed dry- or wet-cooled projects should use water conservation practices.

Wildlife (mammals): The fencing around the solar energy development should not block the free movement of mammals, particularly big game species.

Cultural resources: Coordination with the trail administration for the Old Spanish Trail and Old Spanish Trail Association is recommended for identifying potential mitigation strategies for avoiding or minimizing potential impacts on the congressionally designated Old Spanish National Historic Trail and also on any remnants of the National Register of Historic Places-listed sites associated with the Old Spanish Trail/Mormon Road that may be located within the SEZ. Avoidance of the Old Spanish Trail site within the southeastern portion of the proposed SEZ is recommended.

Native American concerns: The Moapa Band of Paiute Indians have specifically requested formal government-to-government contact when construction or land management projects are being proposed on and/or near the Muddy River, Virgin River, Colorado River, Arrow Canyon Range, Potato Woman, and Apex Pleistocene Lake. Compensatory programs of mitigation could be implemented to provide access to and/or deliberately cultivate patches of culturally significant plants within the Dry Lake SEZ or on other public lands nearby where tribes have ready access. The BLM should consider assisting the Moapa Band of Paiute Indians with the preparation of forms to nominate identified sacred places as traditional cultural properties, if it is found that all the proper eligibility requirements are met.

Some additional minimization measures would likely be identified during preparation of a NEPA analysis to support a competitive lease offering within the SEZ. These measures would also be incorporated into the lease offering as stipulations. For example, if any archaeological sites are found during the cultural resource inventory (see text box titled Dry Lake Cultural Resources) and are determined to be eligible for listing in the National Register of Historic Places, onsite mitigation or avoidance strategies will be considered during consultation with the BLM-Nevada state historic preservation officer and affected tribes to minimize impacts on significant cultural resources.

2.4.3 Regional Mitigation

Identifying the impacts of utility-scale solar development that may warrant regional mitigation involves three steps: (1) identifying all the potential impacts; (2) identifying which of the potential impacts are likely to be unavoidable (i.e., the impacts that cannot be mitigated onsite by avoidance and/or the implementation of design features meant to minimize the impact); and (3) identifying which of the unavoidable impacts may warrant regional mitigation by taking into consideration the condition and trend of the impacted resources in the region and how they could be affected by the unavoidable impacts.

As part of the Dry Lake SRMS process, a team of specialists from the BLM Southern Nevada District Office (called the interdisciplinary team) reevaluated the potential impacts of solar development that were described in the Final Solar PEIS (see Section 2.3) in the light of available data specific to the SEZ area. This team, along with other BLM subject matter experts and Argonne National Laboratory subject matter experts, followed the methodology presented in Sections 2.4.3.1 and 2.4.3.2 for first identifying unavoidable impacts from solar development in the SEZ, and then for identifying the unavoidable impacts that may warrant regional mitigation.

Dry Lake Cultural Resources

Following the process for evaluating cultural resources outlined in Appendix E of the BLM technical reference, titled "Procedural Guidance for Developing Solar Regional Mitigation Strategies" the BLM interdisciplinary team determined cultural resources at the Dry Lake SEZ could most likely be mitigated onsite and would not require regional mitigation.

At the time of the pilot Dry Lake SEZ Solar Regional Mitigation Planning Project, a relatively high percentage of the Dry Lake SEZ (well over 20%) had been previously surveyed and/or had been previously disturbed during other industrial activities (e.g., power generation, transmission, mining/milling) with few known sites recorded. A segment of the Old Spanish Trail/Mormon Road (not identified as part of the congressionally designated national historic trail) was previously evaluated and determined significant; it is listed as part of a National Register historic district. Because of its proximity to two washes already established as avoidance areas and a set of existing transmission line rights-of-way, it was determined by the interdisciplinary team that any potential impacts on the cultural site (road) are "avoidable," and no development with the potential to impact the site would be approved in that portion of the SEZ (see Section 2.4.1.2). No other National Register-eligible sites were known within the SEZ at the time of the pilot. An archaeological inventory of the unsurveyed portions of the SEZ is scheduled to be completed prior to offering the SEZ for competitive lease.

In the case of the pilot, it was determined by the interdisciplinary team that a regional approach to mitigation planning did not make sense for the Dry Lake SEZ because other SEZs would not likely benefit (not in same region) and because little cost savings and efficiency could be gained with so little survey needed. It was also assumed that the few significant sites that might be found in the SEZ during the future inventory could be mitigated most effectively onsite (i.e., within the SEZ) using traditional methods and in consultation with the state historic preservation officer and tribes. The cultural resource mitigation planning for the Dry Lake SEZ was able to be stopped at this point, and it was concluded that standard procedures for addressing cultural resource impacts made the most sense; the standard procedures would complete the inventory and evaluation and mitigate for any significant sites within the SEZ.

In addition, consultation with the Moapa Band of Paiute Indians and other tribes had not identified archaeological/cultural resources significant to them in the SEZ, although resources in the surrounding areas had been identified through an ethnographic study (SWCA and University of Arizona 2011). At the time of the pilot, the BLM was still seeking clarifications from the Moapa on whether portions of the Salt Song Trail or other traditional trails crossed the SEZ and whether cultural resource impacts of interest to the tribe were possible. This issue has not yet been resolved. Based on feedback during the pilot Dry Lake SEZ Solar Regional Mitigation Planning Project workshops, the Moapa were most concerned about impacts on habitat, wildlife, and water use.

2.4.3.1 Identification of Unavoidable Impacts

The following methodology was used to identify unavoidable impacts:

- The interdisciplinary team verified/augmented the affected environment and impacts presented in the Final Solar PEIS (for completeness, reviewed analysis in both the Draft and Final Solar PEIS).
  - Reviewed the affected environment and the direct, indirect, and cumulative impacts for each resource value presented in the Final Solar PEIS.
  - Evaluated whether the description of the affected environment and impacts was comprehensive and accurate and whether more detailed information was available that could influence the description of impacts as provided in the PEIS. Where applicable, new information was documented (see Appendix A, Impact Assessment Summary Table).

- The team verified/augmented the programmatic and SEZ-specific design features presented in Appendix A of the Final Solar PEIS.
  - Reviewed the programmatic and SEZ-specific design features presented in the Final Solar PEIS, determined which design features are applicable to the Dry Lake SEZ, and determined if there are additional measures that could be implemented to avoid and/or minimize impacts onsite. Where applicable, this was

documented (see Appendix A, Impact Assessment Summary Table).

- The team identified the impacts that could be mitigated onsite through avoidance and/or minimization, including the required design features and additional measures described previously.
  - For each resource, the design features and additional avoidance and minimization measures were evaluated as to the degree that they could avoid and minimize the impacts.

- The residual impacts were considered to possibly warrant regional mitigation (see Section 2.4.3.2).

The summary table presented in Appendix A documents the basis for the identification of unavoidable impacts for the Dry Lake SEZ.

2.4.3.2 Unavoidable Impacts that May Warrant Regional Mitigation

2.4.3.2.1 Conceptual Models

A conceptual model or models depicting interrelationships between key ecosystem components, processes, and stressors at the Dry Lake SEZ is needed to evaluate the effectiveness of mitigation investments employed through an SRMS. The Dry Lake SEZ specialist team constructed conceptual models to explain the role that resources, individually and in concert with one another, play in the function of the relevant ecological, social, and cultural systems present in the region. This regional model provided the context to identify critical resources at the local scale. Information sources used for the development of the conceptual model included:

- BLM REAs.
- BLM RMPs.
- Resource specialist expert opinion.
- Nature Conservancy ecoregional assessments.
- Habitat conservation plans.

Additional resources (e.g., other baseline resource surveys, inventories, occurrence records, studies/research, assessments, and plans providing insight into regional conditions and trends; ethnographic studies; BLM, county, or regional land use plans; and federal, state, or local social and economic studies) could be used to refine the models in the future.

Developing conceptual models for the Mojave Basin and Range ecosystem, for solar energy development, and for solar energy development at the Dry Lake SEZ was an iterative process between the BLM and the stakeholders, with a goal of describing in detail the processes essential to sustain the ecosystem and the stressors that influence those processes. These conceptual models are presented in Appendix B.

2.4.3.2.2 Unavoidable Impacts that May Warrant Regional Mitigation

Based on the best available information, conceptual models, assessments, and expert opinion, the Dry Lake specialist team identified at-risk resources and processes in the region that coincided with resources as likely experiencing unavoidable adverse impacts due to solar development within the SEZ. The Sonora-Mojave Creosotebush-White Bursage Desert Scrub community was identified as at risk on the basis of the regional trend analysis described in Section 2.1.3.2. The team estimated how the unavoidable impacts of solar development could affect the condition and trend of the at-risk resource values at both local and regional scales.

For each unavoidable impact, the Dry Lake specialist team identified criteria to help determine at what point the degree of unavoidable impacts might warrant regional mitigation. The criteria/decision point referenced:

a. The relative importance placed on the resource in the land use plan.
b. The rarity, legal status, or state or national policy status of the resource.
c. The resilience of the resource in the face of change and impact.

Next, a team applied the criteria to the assumed full build-out of the SEZ to identify which unavoidable impacts, in the context of the regional setting, may warrant regional mitigation for the Dry Lake SEZ. This list has been reviewed by stakeholders, and their comments have been considered. The process for assessing whether impacts to visual resources at the Dry Lake SEZ may warrant regional mitigation is presented in Appendix C.

2.5 Regional Mitigation Goals

2.5.1 Background on Regional Goals

The regional mitigation described in this strategy is focused on recommending appropriate compensation for the unavoidable impacts of developing the Dry Lake SEZ (i.e., those impacts that cannot be either avoided or minimized onsite and are likely to exacerbate problematic regional trends). For impacts recommended for regional mitigation, the mitigation goal, at the broadest level, is to offset the unavoidable adverse impacts that are expected to occur onsite with actions that improve or protect the impacted resource elsewhere in the region. As detailed in the "Procedural Guidance for Developing Solar Regional Mitigation Strategies" (BLM forthcoming), regional mitigation goals should include consideration of the effectiveness, feasibility, durability, and risk of mitigation locations and actions for compensating for unavoidable impacts in the SEZ.

The unavoidable impacts that may warrant regional mitigation for the Dry Lake SEZ (identified in previous steps in this strategy process) are as follows:

- The loss of desert tortoise habitat and the potential loss of individual desert tortoises. The desert tortoise is listed as a threatened species under the Endangered Species Act.

- The loss of habitat and the potential loss of individual animals for the following BLM special status species:

Gila monster, Mojave Desert sidewinder, ferruginous hawk, golden eagle, loggerhead shrike, and Le Conte's thrasher.

- The loss of rosy two-toned penstemon (also known as pinto beardtongue) habitat and the potential loss of individual plants. The rosy two-toned penstemon is a BLM special status species plant.

- The loss of ecosystem services and the human uses depending on them, as a result of development and until the lease expires and the site is restored. The primary components of an ecological system are: soils, vegetation, water, air, and wildlife.

- The visual impacts that will occur that exceed the allowable level within the portion of the SEZ located within the area designated as visual resource management (VRM) Class III in the Las Vegas RMP (BLM 1998).

In addition, the following unavoidable impacts were identified as having the potential to occur, depending on the way the area is developed, the success of onsite mitigation activities, data gaps, and/or the discovery of unanticipated resources:

- Introduction and spread of invasive/noxious weeds.

- Alterations to surface hydrology.

- Loss of cultural resources.

- Increased density of desert tortoise in the Coyote Springs ACEC (established for tortoise recovery).

- Visual resources as seen from nearby specially designated areas.

- Certain Native American concerns (e.g., loss of habitat and spiritual value).

While no regional mitigation objectives are proposed for these potential impacts, they will be the focus of an elevated level of monitoring so as to facilitate the timely detection of unanticipated impacts and conditional stipulations to be included in the grant to afford prompt and effective remediation.

2.5.2 Las Vegas Resource Management Plan Goals and Objectives

The Las Vegas RMP (BLM 1998) guides BLM project-specific decisions in the region in which the Dry Lake SEZ is located. The Las Vegas RMP established the following management goals and objectives related to the unavoidable impacts identified in 2.5.1 for the Dry Lake SEZ:

Desert Tortoise

- Manage habitat to further sustain the populations of federally listed species so they no longer need protection under the Endangered Species Act.

- Manage desert tortoise habitat to achieve the recovery criteria defined in the "Desert Tortoise (Mojave Population) Recovery Plan" (Brussard et al. 1994) and ultimately to achieve delisting of the desert tortoise.

Special Status Species Animals

- Manage habitats for nonlisted special status species to support viable populations so future listing is not necessary.

Special Status Species Plants

- Manage habitats for nonlisted special status species to support viable populations so future listing is not necessary.

Ecosystem Loss

- Restore plant productivity on disturbed areas of public lands.

- Reduce erosion and sedimentation while maintaining, or where possible, enhancing soil productivity through the maintenance and improvement of watershed conditions.

- Support viable and diverse wildlife populations by providing and maintaining sufficient quality and quantity of food, water, cover, and space to satisfy needs of wildlife species using habitats on public land.

Visual Resources

- Manage (VRM Class III) for partial retention of the existing character of the landscape. In these areas, authorized actions may alter the existing landscape but not to the extent that they attract or focus the attention of the casual viewer.

2.5.3 Dry Lake Solar Energy Zone Mitigation Goals and Objectives

The following Dry Lake SEZ-specific regional mitigation goals and objectives were developed using the "Procedural Guidance for Developing Solar Regional Mitigation Strategies" (BLM forthcoming). They are high-level goals and objectives to be considered in selecting mitigation locations and actions and to serve as a framework for identifying site-specific mitigation goals and objectives (see Section 2.7).

Desert Tortoise

- Goal: Mitigate unavoidable impacts to further sustain the populations of federally listed species so they no longer need protection under the Endangered Species Act.

- Objective: Comply with the permit (Endangered Species Act, Section 7) issued to the BLM by the U.S. Fish and Wildlife Service for disturbance of tortoise habitat in the Southern Nevada District Office RMP area. Collect the Section 7 mitigation fee (currently $824 per acre) for use in supporting the recovery of the species.

Special Status Species Animals

- Goal: Manage habitats for nonlisted special status species to support viable populations so future listing is not necessary.

- Objective: Mitigate the loss of habitat by restoring and/or protecting habitat in the same region in which the SEZ is located.

Special Status Species Plants

- Goal: Mitigate the loss of plants and habitat for the rosy two-toned penstemon to support viable populations in which the SEZ is located so future listing of the plant is not necessary.

- Objective 1: Protect genetic diversity by seed collection before disturbance.

- Objective 2: Secure basic scientific information pertaining to the rosy two-toned penstemon.

Ecosystem Services

- Goal: Restore and/or preserve the creosote-bursage vegetation community disrupted by development (taking into account the existing landscape condition in the SEZ).

- Objective: Restore and/or preserve the creosote-bursage vegetation community and ecosystem proportionate to the condition of this same ecosystem in the Dry Lake SEZ and, where possible, in concert with protection/restoration of special status species (animal and plant) habitat.

Visual Resources

- Goal: Restore and/or protect the visual resource values altered by development of the SEZ (taking into account the existing condition of visual resource values in the Dry Lake SEZ).

- Objective: Restore and/or protect visual resource values proportionate to expected impacts in concert with ecosystem restoration.

2.6 Calculating the Recommended Mitigation Fee for the Dry Lake Solar Energy Zone

The mitigation fee is intended to be a one-time fee paid by a developer for the acres being disturbed by development. While the fee is assessed once, before development commences, it should be administered over the life of the solar project. The actual fee for the Dry Lake SEZ should be developed just prior to leasing. An example calculation of the fee is provided here for illustration purposes.

The regional mitigation fee for the Dry Lake SEZ is calculated according to the "Procedural Guidance for Developing Solar Regional Mitigation Strategies (BLM forthcoming). For the Dry Lake SEZ, the fee can be calculated as follows:

Project mitigation fee =
(number of acres) X
(per acre regional mitigation fee)

The specific methods and values used to calculate the per-acre regional mitigation fee can vary between SEZs and involve a number of different calculations.

Figure 2-9 presents a flow diagram describing the various potential pathways that can be used to calculate the per-acre regional mitigation fee. The example process used at the Dry Lake SEZ is highlighted in yellow in the figure. The steps that follow correspond to Figure 2-9 and outline the calculation of and example regional mitigation fee for the Dry Lake SEZ.

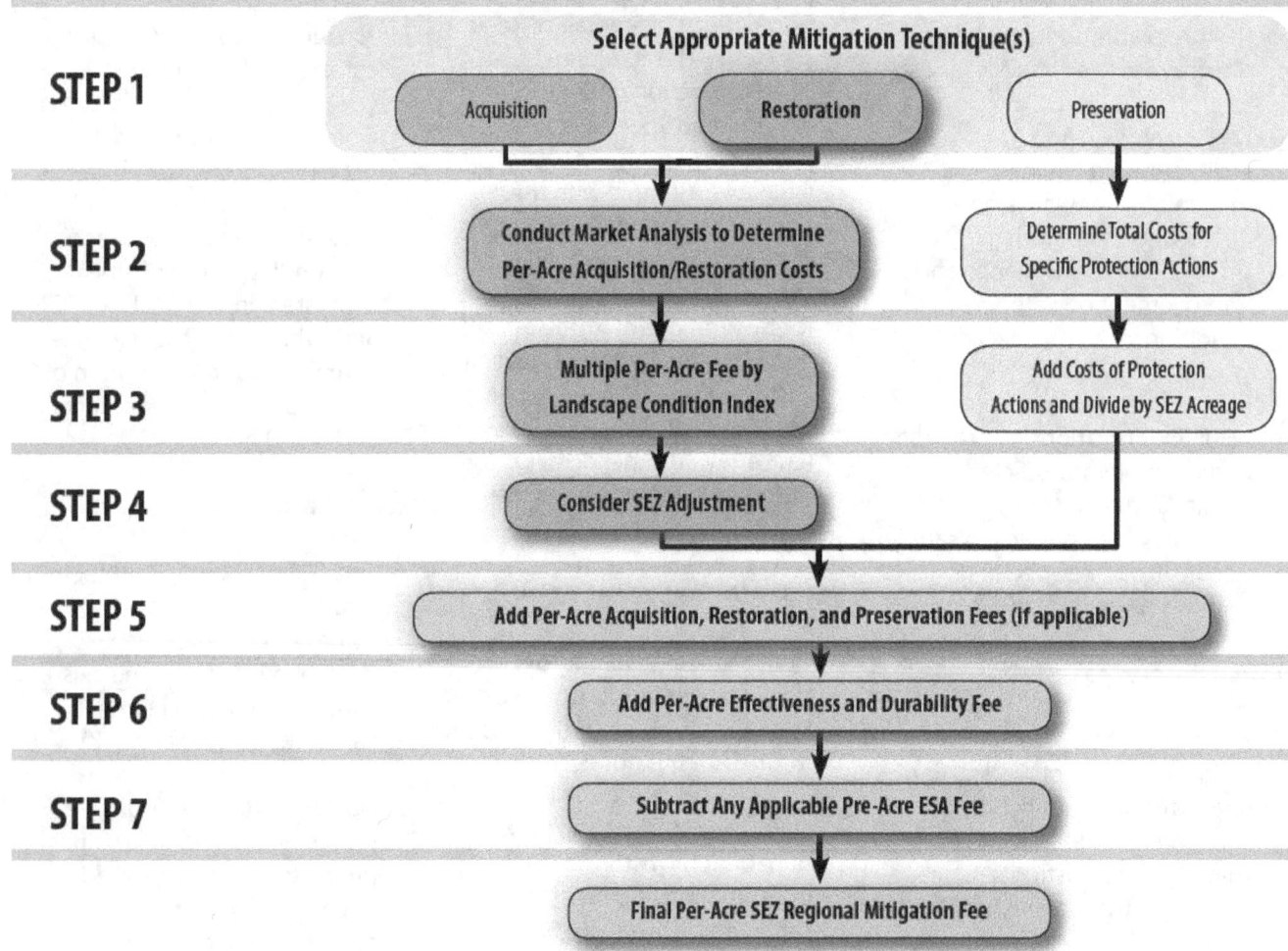

Figure 2-9. Steps for calculating per-acre regional mitigation fees.

Step 1: Select Mitigation Action(s) and Location(s): As described in Section 2.8, the recommended mitigation actions/location are: (1) increase law enforcement and monitoring activities to halt the trend in degradation of resource values; and (2) restore disturbed areas in the Gold Butte ACEC.

Step 2: Calculate the Base Fee: The market analysis for the Dry Lake SEZ mitigation consisted of a BLM economist querying local contractors for the cost of restoring an acre of burn scar to the creosote-bursage vegetative community (the main vegetative community at Dry Lake). The BLM determined that the cost of restoration was roughly $10,000 per acre.

Example: *Base Per-Acre Mitigation Fee = $10,000*

Step 3: Calculate the Adjusted Base Fee: Since the base per-acre mitigation fee calculated in Step 2 represents the costs of restoring a completely altered landscape, it is necessary to adjust the restoration fee to reflect the actual landscape conditions within the SEZ. To do this, the base mitigation fee calculated in Step 2 is multiplied by the landscape condition index, which for the Dry Lake SEZ is 52.8% (NatureServe 2013).

Example: *Adjusted Base Per-Acre Mitigation Fee = ($10,000 x 0.528) = $5,280*

Step 4: Consider SEZ Adjustment: For some SEZs, the BLM may apply an adjustment intended to direct solar development to the SEZ and account for degraded site-specific habitat conditions not considered in Step 3. The BLM may use this discretion, on a case-by-case basis, to identify appropriate terms and conditions—including those relating to mitigation—for FLPMA Title V right-of-way authorizations. The BLM recommends an adjustment of 50% for the Dry Lake SEZ.

Example: *Recommended Dry Lake SEZ Adjusted Base Per-Acre Mitigation Fee = ($5,280 x 0.50) = $2,640*

Step 5: Add Per-Acre Acquisition, Restoration, and Preservation Fees: There are no acquisitions proposed for the Dry Lake SEZ. The costs of increased law enforcement and monitoring are added in Step 6.

Step 6: Add Per-Acre Effectiveness and Durability Fee: To ensure all mitigation techniques chosen in Step 1 are effective and durable, a standard BLM effectiveness and durability fee should be applied to regional mitigation fees. Table 2-4 details how this fee is calculated. This fee is simply added to the per-acre fee calculated in Step 5.

Example: *Recommended Dry Lake SEZ Adjusted Base Per-Acre Mitigation Fee = ($2,640 + $20) = $2,660*

Table 2-4. Estimate of funding needed for management activities to ensure effectiveness and durability[a].

Tasks	Per Acre/ Per Year
Law enforcement	$15
Effectiveness monitoring	$5
TOTAL	$20
Annual rate for 5,000-acre SEZ	$100,000
Total 30-year management fee/5,000-acre SEZ	$3,000,000

[a] The cost estimates were derived from a cursory market analysis and will be finalized once competitive interest is received.

Step 7: Subtract Any Applicable Endangered Species Act Section 7 Fees: The Dry Lake SEZ is in an area subject to Section 7 permitting for the desert tortoise, a species listed under the Endangered Species Act as threatened. The Endangered Species Act Section 7 mitigation fee for Clark County, where the SEZ is located, is $824 per acre. Each developer is required to pay this fee, and the funds are expended in pursuit of species recovery. Because the expenditure of Section 7 fees is consistent with Dry Lake regional mitigation goals and objectives (see Section 2.5.3), the Section 7 mitigation fee is subtracted from the base fee to avoid duplicate payment. The fee amount will still be charged to the developer and expended for mitigation of impacts to desert tortoise in consultation with the U.S. Fish and Wildlife Service.

Example: *Recommended Dry Lake SEZ Per-Acre Mitigation Fee = $2,660 - $824 = $1,836*

2.7 Management of Solar Regional Mitigation Fees

The BLM will select management options for SEZ mitigation fees that are consistent with the BLM's interim policy, draft Manual Section 1794, "Regional Mitigation," issued June 13, 2013, which includes guidance for management of funds collected as part of the restoration, acquisition, or preservation portion of the total mitigation fee by an independent third party.

2.8 Evaluation of Mitigation Locations, Objectives, and Actions

The proposed regional mitigation locations and actions will mitigate for the temporary loss of some of the resources that will occur as a result of solar development in the Dry Lake SEZ (e.g., loss of creosote-bursage vegetation, loss of general and BLM special status species habitat, loss of cryptobiotic soil crusts and desert pavement, and loss of the ecosystem services these resources provide). The BLM Southern Nevada District Office considered several regional mitigation action alternatives. The suite of potential mitigation actions were generated by soliciting proposals from the public and from BLM staff in the district. The proposals included:

- Restoring disturbed land in several ACECs and one national conservation area in the vicinity of the Dry Lake SEZ.

- Preventing further degradation in several ACECs and one national conservation area in the vicinity of the Dry Lake SEZ.

- Acquiring private land in the vicinity of the Dry Lake SEZ and managing it for conservation values.

The following proposed mitigation locations were screened and given a preliminary ranking using criteria based on the regional mitigation goals described in Section 2.5. The results of the ranking are summarized in the screening table for candidate regional mitigation locations for the Dry Lake SEZ (Appendix D):

- Gold Butte ACEC.
- Mormon Mesa ACEC.
- Coyote Springs ACEC.
- Piute-Eldorado Valley ACEC.
- Coyote Springs ACEC, plus adjacent lands as proposed by the The Nature Conservancy.

The following criteria were used to screen and rank these sites:

- The sites are within the Las Vegas Field Office (i.e., the same subregion and landscape context as the Dry Lake SEZ).

- The sites contain the same creosote-bursage vegetation community.

- The sites are within desert tortoise critical habitat. Regional mitigation for the Dry Lake SEZ would indirectly benefit conservation and recovery efforts for the desert tortoise.

- The sites provide habitat for a similar suite of general wildlife, special status wildlife, and rare plants.

- The sites are in a higher VRM class than the Dry Lake SEZ. Improvements provided by regional mitigation for the Dry Lake SEZ would result in improvements to a higher VRM class.

- The degree to which the mitigation site and actions are consistent with the Las Vegas RMP.

- The degree to which applicable management prescriptions in

the Las Vegas RMP (BLM 1998) facilitate durable mitigation investments. Management prescriptions that facilitate durability include, but are not limited to: special conservation-oriented designations, such as national conservation areas, ACECs, designated wilderness areas, and wilderness study areas; areas where land-disturbing activities are prohibited; and areas where land-disturbing activities are discouraged.

Proposed Mitigation Actions and Locations. The Gold Butte ACEC is preliminarily recommended as the best recipient location for regional mitigation from the Dry Lake SEZ. This ACEC is located 32 miles (51 km) east of the Dry Lake SEZ (see Figure 2-10). This ACEC is recommended based on the following reasons:

- The Mojave Basin and Range REA (NatureServe 2013) suggests that creosote-bursage vegetation in the Gold Butte ACEC may persist longer under climate change than the other nominated ACECs.

- Niche modeling, completed by the National Park Service for the Lake Mead National Recreation Area, suggests, under future climate change, high-quality desert tortoise habitat will remain in the Gold Butte ACEC while most of the adjacent desert tortoise habitat in the national recreation area will decline and disappear.

- Road decommissioning and restoration is proposed as a Dry Lake SEZ regional mitigation activity. The Gold Butte ACEC has already completed road designations. Road designations have not been completed on the other ACECs.

- Reseeding burn scars is proposed as a Dry Lake SEZ regional mitigation activity. The Gold Butte ACEC suffered multiple wildfires in 2005 and 2006 and could benefit from restoration. The other ACECs have had fewer fires.

- The Gold Butte ACEC is an important landscape corridor between Lake Mead and the Virgin Mountains for game species managed by the Nevada Department of Wildlife.

The Gold Butte ACEC was established in the Las Vegas RMP (BLM 1998). It has an area of approximately 350,000 acres (1416 km²). The primary resource values listed in the RMP are:

- Cultural and historic resources.
- Scenic values.
- Wildlife habitat.
- Special status species habitat.
- Botanical resources.

The Las Vegas RMP also specifies the resource constraints of the Gold Butte ACEC, which include:

- Closed to mineral entry, sale, and leasing, except for fluid minerals under certain circumstances.

- Closed to grazing.
- Managed for wild burros at an appropriate management level of 98 animals.
- Off-road vehicle use limited to existing roads and trails.
- Closed to off-road vehicle events.
- Right-of-way avoidance.

The resource values found in the Gold Butte ACEC are threatened by: unauthorized activities, including off-road vehicle use, illegal dumping, and trespass livestock grazing; wildfire; and weed infestation. Existing burned areas, unauthorized roads and trails, and areas disturbed by other activities await funding for rehabilitation. Neutralizing these threats and restoring altered ecological systems are the focus of the regional mitigation proposed for this area.

Two action-specific mitigation goals and nine mitigation objectives are recommended to be undertaken to compensate for the unavoidable impacts associated with the development of the Dry Lake SEZ (see Table 2-5). Some of these objectives are associated with preventing degradation in the Gold Butte ACEC. The total cost of affecting the protection of this ACEC for 30 years, the expected term of a solar development right-of-way, is about $9 million. The Gold Butte ACEC is about 350,000 acres, and the cost is about $25.92 per acre. The total mitigation fee expected to be collected for the Dry Lake SEZ if full build-out of the 3,591 developable acres in the SEZ occurs is approximately $6.6 million (see Section 2.6). Mitigation

funds from a single SEZ will not likely be the only source of funding for a given regional mitigation effort, such as restoration in the Gold Butte ACEC. State and federal agencies, including the BLM, should identify opportunities for pooling financial resources from additional developments required to implement regional mitigation actions.

The restoration goals in the Gold Butte ACEC are to:

1. Prevent further degradation of the ACEC, and ensure the durability of the conservation investment by:
   a. Augmenting BLM law enforcement capacity sufficient to maintain ranger patrols in the ACEC.
   b. Providing a monitor to track activities in and impacts to the ACEC.
   c. Building the capacity to respond in a timely manner to activities that threaten resource values.
   d. Providing treatment for noxious weeds and maintaining fuel breaks to protect the area.

2. Restoring creosote-bursage vegetation on closed roads, burn scars, and other anthropogenic impacts. Included in this goal is the procurement of genetically appropriate native seed to complete these restoration activities.

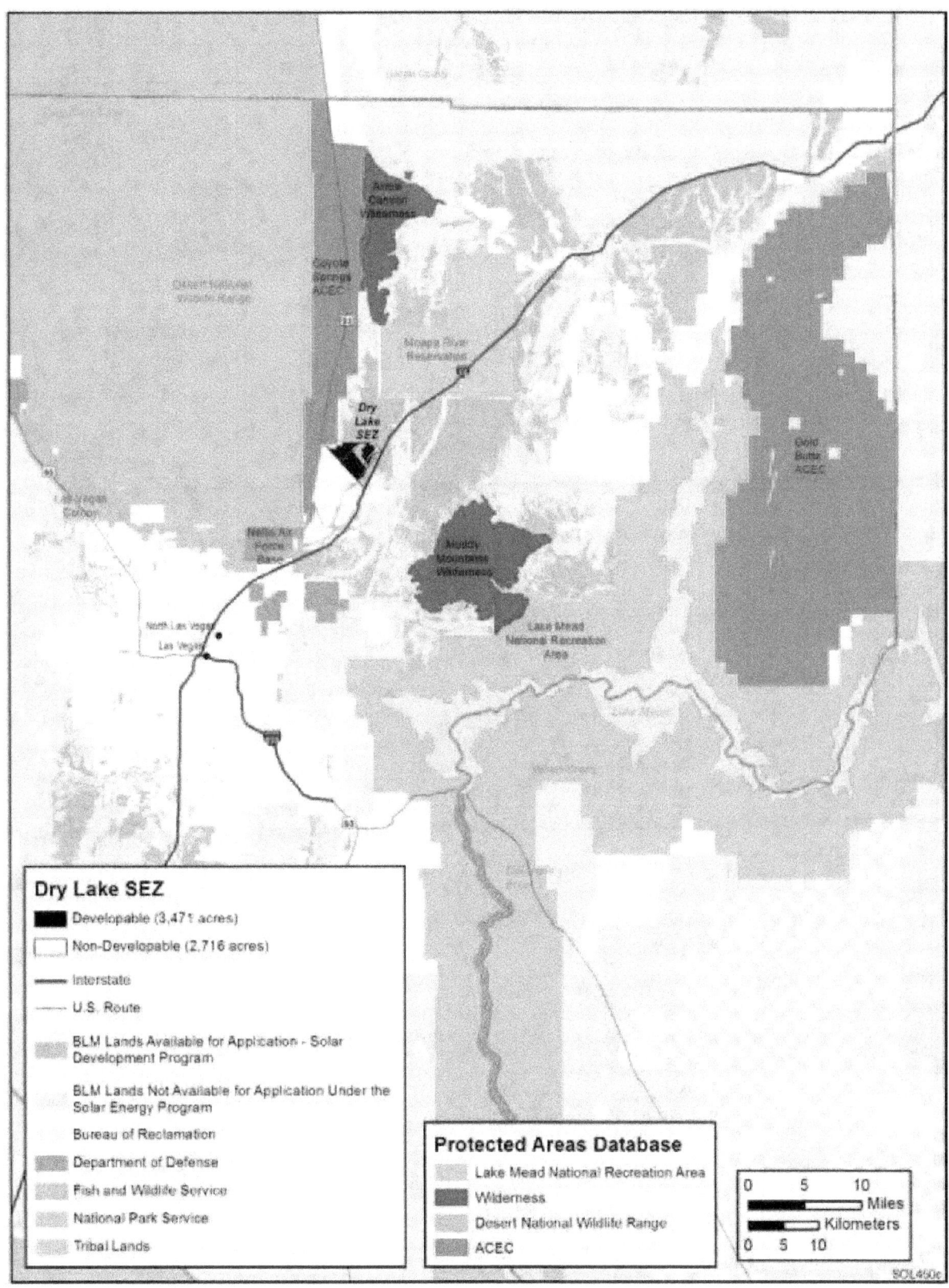

Dry Lake SEZ

■ Developable (3,471 acres)

□ Non-Developable (2,716 acres)

── Interstate

── U.S. Route

BLM Lands Available for Application - Solar Development Program

BLM Lands Not Available for Application Under the Solar Energy Program

Bureau of Reclamation

Department of Defense

Fish and Wildlife Service

National Park Service

Tribal Lands

Protected Areas Database

Lake Mead National Recreation Area

Wilderness

Desert National Wildlife Range

ACEC

0   5   10 Miles

0   5   10 Kilometers

SOL460c

Figure 2-10. Gold Butte Area of Critical Environmental Concern.

Table 2-5. Dry Lake Solar Energy Zone goals and objectives associated with mitigation in the Gold Butte Area of Critical Environmental Concern.

Mitigation Goals and Tasks	Reason Why Mitigation Funds May Be Needed	Measurable Objectives	Indicators
Goal 1: Prevent further degradation of the ACEC, and ensure the durability of the conservation investment in the Gold Butte ACEC.	The purpose of Goal 1 is to address the primary long-term threats to any ACEC that is selected as a recipient site for Dry Lake SEZ regional mitigation. Addressing these long-term impacts will provide the durability requested by the public.	Increase acreage of healthy lands, and decrease unauthorized use and other disturbances.	Acres of disturbed and untreated land in the Gold Butte ACEC (measured annually). Breakout by type of disturbance: wildfire, illegal dumping, unauthorized off-highway vehicle use, unauthorized campsites, noxious weed incursion, etc. Acres of treated land in the ACEC (treated, but has not reached a condition to be considered restored). Breakout by type of treatment.
Task 1.1: Augment law enforcement.	Law enforcement staff is limited within the BLM. Instead of dedicated base funding, law enforcement officers (LEOs) are funded out of benefitting programs (such as wildlife, range, and forestry). With limited funding, BLM program managers must choose between implementing mandated activities and funding LEOs. In the Southern Nevada District, there are six rangers outside of the Red Rock Canyon National Conservation Area. Providing regional mitigation to fund one LEO dedicated to patrol the ACEC is an effective way to manage public use and ensure compliance with area resource management objectives, such as those that protect cultural and historic resources, scenic values, wildlife habitat, special status species habitat, and botanical resources.	After establishing the baseline, reduce the number of incidents in 5 years by 75% and in 10 years by 90%, with a goal of 0 incidents.	Number and nature of incidents of noncompliance. Number of sites and resources protected by law enforcement. Note: With a greater law enforcement presence, the number of reported incidents may increase at first. Will need to normalize data to compensate.
Task 1.2: Monitor small disturbances from anthropogenic impacts (such as off-highway vehicle incursions, dump sites, campsites, and target shooting areas) and treat with signs, fencing, restoration, etc.	Monitoring and responding quickly to small disturbances is the best way to limit their size and extent while positively shaping public use. Current resource management demands on staff time limit the BLM's ability to respond to minor impacts quickly before they grow into larger problems.	Reduce the number of incidents and increase the response time, once a baseline for incidents and response time has been established.	Number of incidents of "small disturbances." Note: The number of reported incidents may increase with increased level of monitoring. Need to normalize data to compensate. Number of rapid responses to disturbances (breakout by type of disturbance).
Task 1.3: Monitor and treat noxious weeds.	Noxious weeds, such as Sahara mustard, are a significant threat to Mojave Desert ecosystems. Monitoring roads and trails and responding quickly to incipient weed populations is the only way to preserve intact ecosystems and prevent large infestations that cannot be treated. BLM funding to accomplish this task is limited.	Reduce the presence of noxious weeds by X% in Y years—a measurable objective can be set after establishing a baseline.	Acreage of noxious weeds (measured annually). Number of weed monitoring reports. Number and acres of weed treatments (measured annually or seasonally).
Task 1.4: Implement, monitor, and maintain fuel breaks.	Fire is a significant threat to Mojave Desert ecosystems. Constructing fuel breaks that work in concert with natural and manmade barriers is an important way to compartmentalize and protect intact vegetation and Mojave ecosystems from large-scale fires, similar to the fires southern Nevada experienced in 2005.	Reduce incidence and spread of fires.	Number of fires and cause. Acreage of lands affected by fire. Number and nature of fuel reduction projects.
Task 1.5: Monitor and periodically evaluate land health and management effectiveness.	Periodically monitoring and evaluating the effectiveness of resource management is a critical part of long-term adaptive management. Monitoring any recipient site will need to be a part of Dry Lake Solar Energy Zone regional mitigation.	Meet rangeland health assessment objectives.	Refer to rangeland health assessment indicators.
Goal 2: Restore creosote-bursage vegetation and the ecosystem services it provides on closed roads, burn scars, and other anthropogenic disturbances within the Gold Butte ACEC.	There are two important reasons why regional mitigation funding should be used to meet Goal 2: (1) There is not dedicated BLM base funding to decommission roads and trails that have been closed through designations; and (2) Emergency stabilization and rehabilitation funding is not appropriate for nonemergency restoration projects, and burned area rehabilitation funding is limited to 3 to 5 years. This timeframe is not practical given Mojave Desert recovery times. Currently, restoration needs go unmet or are funded inconsistently through one-time and soft money opportunities. The collection and use of regional mitigation funds to restore roads and other disturbed sites (such as old burn scars) would not replace BLM base funding.	Increase acreage of land treated.	Acres of disturbed and untreated creosote-bursage vegetation in the Gold Butte ACEC (measured annually). Breakout by type of disturbance: wildfire, illegal dumping, unauthorized off-highway vehicle use, unauthorized campsites, noxious weed incursion, etc. Acres of land treated to restore creosote-bursage vegetation in the ACEC (treated, but has not reached a condition to be considered restored).
Task 2.1: Secure locally appropriate native seed needed for restoration work.	This is a critical task. Using locally sourced seed is the best way to preserve the genetic integrity of existing native plant communities and ensure the best restoration outcome. Preventing genetic erosion and preserving population genetics is one of the best ways to maintain ecosystem resilience from disturbance and adaptation to climate change.		Quantity of native seed collected, purchased, and stockpiled.

Mitigation Goals and Tasks	Reason Why Mitigation Funds May Be Needed	Measurable Objectives	Indicators
Action Item 2.1.1: Collect wildland seed.	This action item is critical to Task 2.1: Collecting and stockpiling modest amounts of native seed each year is the best way to ensure a stable supply of seed for restoration and fire rehabilitation. Under cold storage, the seed of many Mojave Desert species can remain viable for decades. The BLM recently completed construction of a regional native seed warehouse for this purpose.	Increase amount of native seed locally collected and stored.	Quantity of native seed collected and stockpiled.
Action Item 2.1.2: Collect an increased amount of seed by contracting with a commercial vendor.	This action item is critical to Task 2.1.1: Native forbs are extremely important for general wildlife, forage for desert tortoise, supporting native pollinator populations, and ecosystem function. It is not possible and too expensive to collect most native forbs in the quantities needed for restoration. Contracting with a commercial vendor to increase seed from wild collections and stockpile it, is the best way to ensure its availability for the restoration and rehabilitation work.	Increase amount of native seed purchased.	Quantity of native forb seed purchased. Quantity of purchased native forb seed stockpiled.
Task 2.2: Restore closed roads.	The decommissioning and restoration of closed roads meets the regional mitigation needs for impacts to vegetation and ecosystem services described in Goal 2. Closing and rehabilitating roads, by first decompacting soils followed by seeding native species, is an important way to restore landscape connectivity to native plant communities, reduce edge effect, and increase ecosystem resistance to colonization by nonnative weeds.	Reduce the acreage of closed roads by increasing the acreage of closed roads treated to restore native vegetation.	Miles and acres of closed and untreated roads in the Gold Butte ACEC (measured annually). Miles and acres of treated roads (treated, but has not reached a condition to be considered restored). Miles and acres of restored roads in the ACEC.
Task 2.3: Restore new burns and old burn scars.	Reseeding burn scars is an important way to speed up long recovery times. Historically, large wildfires did not occur in the Mojave Desert; the Mojave is not adapted to fire and is very slow to recover from it. Postfire seeding with native species is one way to increase recovery of burned creosote-bursage vegetation.	Decrease acreage of burn scars. Conduct postfire seeding with native species immediately.	Acres of disturbed and untreated land in the Gold Butte ACEC (measured annually) that were disturbed by fire. Acres of treated land in the ACEC (treated, but has not reached a condition to be considered restored). Breakout by type of treatment. For new fires, number of days after the fire that seeding occurred.
Task 2.4: To the extent practicable, salvage and re-inoculate cryptobiotic crusts of disturbed sites to improve soils condition on restoration sites.	On small-scale restoration sites, it is possible to salvage and re-inoculate disturbed areas in order to facilitate recovery. This action directly improves soil resources as a regional mitigation for impacts to cryptobiotic soil crusts within the Dry Lake Solar Energy Zone.	Improve soil condition of restoration sites.	Amount of Dry Lake Solar Energy Zone soil that is salvaged. Number and size (acres) of sites re-inoculated with salvaged soils.

The mitigation activities described in Section 2.8 represent only a part of the funding required to manage the Gold Butte ACEC. Further, achieving these mitigation activities will take more funding than could be accomplished by the regional mitigation fees generated by leasing the Dry Lake SEZ. In order to achieve the mitigation objectives, ensure their durability, and otherwise manage the resource values in the Gold Butte ACEC, the BLM would "pool" funding from several potential sources, including, but not limited to:

- Funding appropriated by Congress for management of the Gold Butte ACEC.

- Funding collected under the "Final Clark County Multiple Species Habitat Conservation Plan and Environmental Impact Statement for Issuance of a Permit to Allow Incidental Take of 79 Species in Clark County, Nevada" and allocated to the BLM for use in the Gold Butte ACEC.

- Funding derived by land sales conducted under the Southern Nevada Public Land Management Act and allocated to the BLM for conservation initiatives and/or capital improvements in the Gold Butte ACEC.

- Mitigation fees collected for other land-disturbing activities.

Generally, the regional mitigation goals, tasks, and actions described in Table 2-6 are listed in the order they are recommended to occur as funding becomes available. The logic in this sequence is to secure the enforcement infrastructure to prevent further disturbance and ensure durability before undertaking restoration activities.

Table 2-6. Priority/order of Gold Butte Area of Critical Environmental Concern mitigation goals and objectives.

Goal	Task	Action Item	Description	Priority/ Order
1			Prevent further degradation of the ACEC, and ensure the durability of the conservation investment in the Gold Butte ACEC.	
	1		Augment law enforcement.	1
	2		Monitor and treat (with signs, fencing, restoration, etc.) anthropogenic impacts (such as off-highway vehicle incursions, dump sites, campsites, and target shooting areas).	2
	3		Monitor and treat noxious weeds.	3
	4		Implement, monitor, and maintain fuel breaks.	4
2			Restore creosote-bursage vegetation and the ecosystem services it provides on closed roads, burn scars, and other anthropogenic disturbances within the Gold Butte ACEC.	
	1		Secure locally appropriate native seed needed for restoration work.	5
		1	Collect wildland seed.	6
		2	Collect an increased amount of seed by contracting with a commercial vendor.	7
	2		Restore closed roads.	8
	3		Restore new burns and old burn scars.	9
	4		To the extent practicable, salvage and re-inoculate cryptobiotic crusts of disturbed sites to improve soils condition on restoration sites.	simultaneous with 8 and 9

2.9 Mitigation Effectiveness Monitoring and Adaptive Management Plan

In the Final Solar PEIS, the BLM committed to developing and incorporating a monitoring and adaptive management plan into its solar energy program. The BLM "Assessment, Inventory, and Monitoring Strategy for Integrated Renewable Resources Management" (AIM Strategy) (Toevs et al. 2011) will guide the development of a Dry Lake monitoring plan that will inform management questions at multiple scales of inquiry (e.g., the land use plan area, mitigation area, project area, and treatment). Detailed information about how the AIM Strategy will be implemented to support long-term monitoring of solar development is provided in Appendix A, Section A.2.4 of the Final Solar PEIS. This monitoring plan will also be consistent with and complement the BLM regional and national monitoring activities.

In the context of solar energy development, long-term monitoring should be conducted to (1) evaluate the effectiveness of mitigation measures, including avoidance measures, onsite mitigation, and regional mitigation; (2) detect unanticipated direct and cumulative impacts at the project and regional level; and (3) evaluate the effectiveness of elements of the BLM's solar energy program (e.g., policies, design features). To ensure that investments in regional mitigation actions are effective and that regional mitigation goals and objectives are being met, it is critical that the long-term monitoring plan include monitoring objectives specific to the regional mitigation locations and actions. The findings of the long-term monitoring activities will be examined by the BLM to support adaptive management of solar development (i.e., to identify the need to adjust operational parameters, modify mitigation measures, and/or implement new mitigation to prevent or minimize further impacts). The following steps will be conducted to develop the mitigation effectiveness monitoring plan for the Dry Lake SEZ:

Step 1. Developed Management Questions and Monitoring Goals.

The BLM interdisciplinary team developed management questions to articulate the issues of concern related to monitoring mitigation effectiveness. The management questions provide the basis for developing monitoring goals. The management questions and monitoring goals for the Dry Lake SEZ are provided in the two text boxes that follow.

Management Questions Established for the Dry Lake Solar Regional Mitigation Strategy

1. Were the design features of the solar development effective to contain the impact of solar installation to the project site (e.g., trend of attributes, special status species habitat indicators, invasive species, habitat metrics)?

2. Are the avoidance areas maintaining ecological composition and process similar to those adjacent to the project area?

3. Did the regional mitigation actions achieve their objectives?

4. Were the Dry Lake Solar Energy Zone (SEZ) mitigation actions, collectively, effective in improving the trend of rangeland health attributes and landscape metrics in the regional mitigation site(s)?

5. What is the status and trend of rangeland health attributes for critical ecological processes necessary to sustain the Mojave Desert ecosystem at three scales: the Dry Lake SEZ 2-mile buffer area, the mitigation area(s), and the Mojave Basin and Range ecoregion? (Note: Some impacts may need to be assessed at different distances (e.g., watershed, airshed).)

Monitoring Goals Established for the Dry Lake Solar Regional Mitigation Strategy

1. Establish baseline measurements of rangeland health and landscape pattern.

2. Determine the status, condition, and trend of priority resources, rangeland health attributes, and landscape pattern metrics once the permitted activity and related mitigation actions have been implemented.

3. Leverage the quantitative data from goals 1 and 2 to map the location, amount, and spatial pattern of priority resources and disturbances.

4. Generate quantitative and spatial data to address goals 1 and 2 and to contribute to existing land health assessment and evaluation processes at multiple scales of inquiry.

5. Generate quantitative and spatial data to determine if management actions (e.g., stipulations, land treatments) are moving resources toward desired states, conditions, or specific resource objectives identified in planning or related documents or legal mandates.

6. Use the collected data to validate and refine the conceptual understanding of key ecosystem components, processes, and sustainability concepts for the Mojave Basin and Range ecoregion and the Dry Lake SEZ.

Step 2. Identify Measureable Monitoring Objectives and Indicators.

Measureable monitoring objectives will be established for each monitoring goal identified in Step 1. Objective setting will be based on current regulatory requirements, RMP goals, or the desired future condition consistent with the land potential (as described in the ecological site description, if available – see Step 4). Examples of measureable monitoring objectives are provided in the text box titled Measureable Monitoring Objective Examples.

Measureable Monitoring Objective Examples

An example of a measureable objective for land status/trend of vegetation is:

(1) Detect a difference of 10 percentage points in the average amount of bare ground in the <MITIGATION LOCATION> over a 5-year period with 90% confidence.

(2) Determine whether cover of perennial grasses in the <MITIGATION LOCATION> is at least 25% with 90% confidence.

An example of an objective for special status species is:

(1) Ensure that populations of <SPECIAL STATUS SPECIES NAME> in the <ECOREGION NAME> have not decreased by more than 20% within 5 years of the solar installation with 95% confidence.

Objective setting includes specifying the attribute and measurable indicators of those attributes to be monitored. Monitoring objectives will indicate the desired amount of change (specific), level of confidence for the measured change (measurable), funding and capacity requirements (achievable), relationship to the management question (relevant), and timeframe during which the measurement occurs to effectively inform management (time sensitive).

Indicator selection will start with the standard AIM core and contingent quantitative indicators

(MacKinnon et al. 2011) and supplement with additional indicators derived from ecosystem conceptual models and/or linked to specific management questions. The AIM core indicators and methods provide high-quality, quantitative information on all land cover types the BLM manages (MacKinnon et al. 2011). Table 2-7 (reproduced from MacKinnon et al. (2011)) lists each method and the corresponding indicators it measures, and the table describes recommendations to achieve consistent implementation across the BLM. When an ecological site at a monitoring location is identified, the BLM core measurements can be assessed in concert with information contained in the ecological site descriptions and the accompanying state and transition model to ascertain departure from an expected reference condition. The methodology for this assessment is contained in "Interpreting Indicators of Rangeland Health," BLM Technical Reference 1734-6. Table 2-8 is a summary table from this technical reference.

Table 2-7. Recommended methods and measurements for core and contingent indicators (reproduced from MacKinnon et al. (2011)).

Method	Indicator(s)	Description
For core indicators		
Line-point intercept with plot-level species inventory	• Bare ground • Vegetation composition • Nonnative invasive species • Plant species of management concern	Line-point intercept (LPI) is a rapid and accurate method for quantifying cover of vegetation and bare ground. Because LPI can underestimate cover of uncommon species, this method is supplemented with searches of a 150-ft (45.7-m) diameter standard plot for at least 15 minutes and until new species detections are more than 2 minutes apart. When performing LPI within tree cover, a modified pin method (e.g., a pivot-table laser or extendable pin) will be used to capture overstory cover.
Vegetation height measurement	• Vegetation height	Measure height of tallest leaf or stem of woody and herbaceous vegetation (living or dead) within a 6-in (15-cm) radius recorded for points along a transect. If vegetation is taller than 10 ft, a standard tape and clinometer method should be used to estimate vegetation height.
Canopy gap intercept	• Proportion of soil surface in large intercanopy gaps	Canopy gap intercept measures the proportion of a line covered by large gaps between plant canopies and is an important indicator of the potential for erosion. Use 1-ft (30-cm) minimum gaps.
For contingent indicators		
Soil stability test	• Soil aggregate stability	This test measures the soil's stability when exposed to rapid wetting and provides information on integrity of soil aggregates, degree of structural development, resistance to erosion, and soil biotic integrity.
Soil sample collection and analysis	• Significant accumulation of soil toxins	The presence and concentrations of toxins are assessed by collecting three samples from the soil surface and one sample at depths of 0 to 4 in (0 to 10 cm) and 4 to 8 in (10 to 20 cm) using a soil corer and following Forest Inventory and Analysis protocol.

Table 2-8. Quantitative indicators and measurements relevant to each of the three rangeland health attributes (reproduced from Pellant et al. (2005)).

Attribute	Qualitative Assessment Indicator	Quantitative Measurement Method	Key Quantitative Assessment Indicator
Soil/site stability	• Rills • Water flow patterns • Pedestals and/or terracettes • Bare ground • Gullies • Wind-scoured, blowout, and/or depositional areas • Litter movement • Soil surface resistance to erosion • Soil surface loss or degradation • Compaction layer	Line-point intercept	Bare ground
		Canopy gap intercept	Proportion of soil surface covered by canopy gaps longer than a defined minimum
		Soil stability test	Soil macro-aggregate stability in water
Hydrologic function	• Rills • Water flow patterns • Pedestals and/or terracettes • Bare ground • Gullies • Soil surface resistance to erosion • Soil surface loss or degradation • Plant community composition and distribution relative to infiltration and runoff • Compaction layer • Litter amount	Line-point intercept	Bare ground
		Canopy gap intercept	Proportion of soil surface covered by canopy gaps longer than a defined minimum
		Soil stability test	Soil macro-aggregate stability in water
Biotic integrity	• Soil surface resistance to erosion • Soil surface loss or degradation • Compaction layer • Functional/structural groups • Plant mortality/decadence • Litter amount • Annual production • Invasive plants • Reproductive capability of perennial plants	Soil stability test	Soil macro-aggregate stability in water
		Line-point intercept	Plant canopy (foliar) cover by functional group
		Line-point intercept	Plant basal cover by functional group
		Line-point intercept	Litter cover
		Line-point intercept	Invasive plant cover

In addition to the BLM core indicators, the BLM will consider requiring dust and noise monitoring as a leasing stipulation for the Dry Lake SEZ. The developer's proposal will be reviewed by the BLM monitoring team to evaluate the efficacy of the proposal in complying with permit stipulations and informing BLM regulatory and land management needs.

Special Status Plant Species Monitoring. The BLM will consider requiring the developer to fund the seed collection and long-term storage of any special status species plant population found on the project site and to conduct long-term monitoring on populations found on the project site and located in the same geographic region for the length of the duration of the impact. A special status plant species monitoring plan will be designed to determine the status, trend, and recruitment success of the populations and will follow methods described in BLM Technical Reference 1730-1, "Measuring and Monitoring Plant Populations" (Elzinga, Salzer, and Willoughby 1998).

Step 3. Develop Sampling Schema.

Based on the management questions, monitoring goals, measurable objectives, and the indicators developed in Steps 1 and 2, the BLM interdisciplinary team will determine the temporal and spatial scale of data collection activities. To develop the sampling schema, the following work will be conducted:

Develop a Statistically Valid and Scalable Sampling Design. Ecological sites are areas of land with the potential to produce similar types and amounts of vegetation based on soils and climate, and ecological sites are the basic units for stratifying landscapes for BLM monitoring activities. Because ecological site descriptions describe the ecological states (plant communities) that can occur in an ecological site and can provide expected indicator values for reference states, they are the foundation upon which BLM monitoring data are evaluated. These data are also fundamental for terrestrial upland land health standards and land health evaluations. Where ecological site descriptions have not been developed, land potential metrics can be developed using a combination of field and remote sensing data to describe current and potential future conditions at broad scales.

Incorporate Status and Trend Monitoring. The monitoring locations are determined through a statistically based (i.e., randomized) selection of monitoring sites. Once the monitoring extent (i.e., inference area) is determined for each scale, a stratified random technique will be used to select monitoring sites such that every location within the monitoring extent has a known and nonzero probability of being selected for sampling. Strata will be based on ecological sites (or groupings of similar ecological sites) to allow for adequate representation of all ecological sites and linear features (e.g., ephemeral washes). See Figure 2-11 for the sampling schema of the Dry Lake SEZ and the 2-mile buffer area. The allocation of sample sites

in the monitoring inference area is determined by the relative area of the stratum with a minimum of three monitoring locations per stratum. Sample sufficiency analysis will be completed for each stratum after the first season of sampling to determine if more monitoring locations are needed in a stratum.

Incorporate Monitoring of Effectiveness of Actions. The sampling schema for an implementation action follows the criterion from the previous paragraph, with the sample population based on the geospatial footprint of the project area and the addition of control sites to determine effectiveness of the action. Control sites are chosen outside of the action area based on similarity of soils and existing vegetation community in the action area. Control sites can be a selection from existing statistically valid monitoring efforts such as the long-term monitoring sites that are a part of the BLM Landscape Monitoring Framework. An example of BLM Landscape Monitoring Framework monitoring sites is represented in Figure 2-12 for the Gold Butte ACEC, which is one of the potential solar

regional mitigation areas in the Dry Lake SRMS.

To account for the variability among sites of similar potential, a minimum of three control sites are selected for each strata present in the treatment area. Sample sufficiency analysis should be conducted after the first year of sampling to examine indicator variability within each stratum to determine if additional sites are needed in the implementation action or control areas.

Integrate Remote Sensing Monitoring Technologies. Considerable work has been done to develop methodologies for processing and analyzing remote sensing data in order to extract information suitable for assessing changes in certain environmental conditions over time. The AIM Strategy emphasizes the value of integrating remote sensing technologies into long-term monitoring programs, wherever feasible, in order to provide cost-effective methods for collecting data and analyzing effects (Toevs et al. 2011).

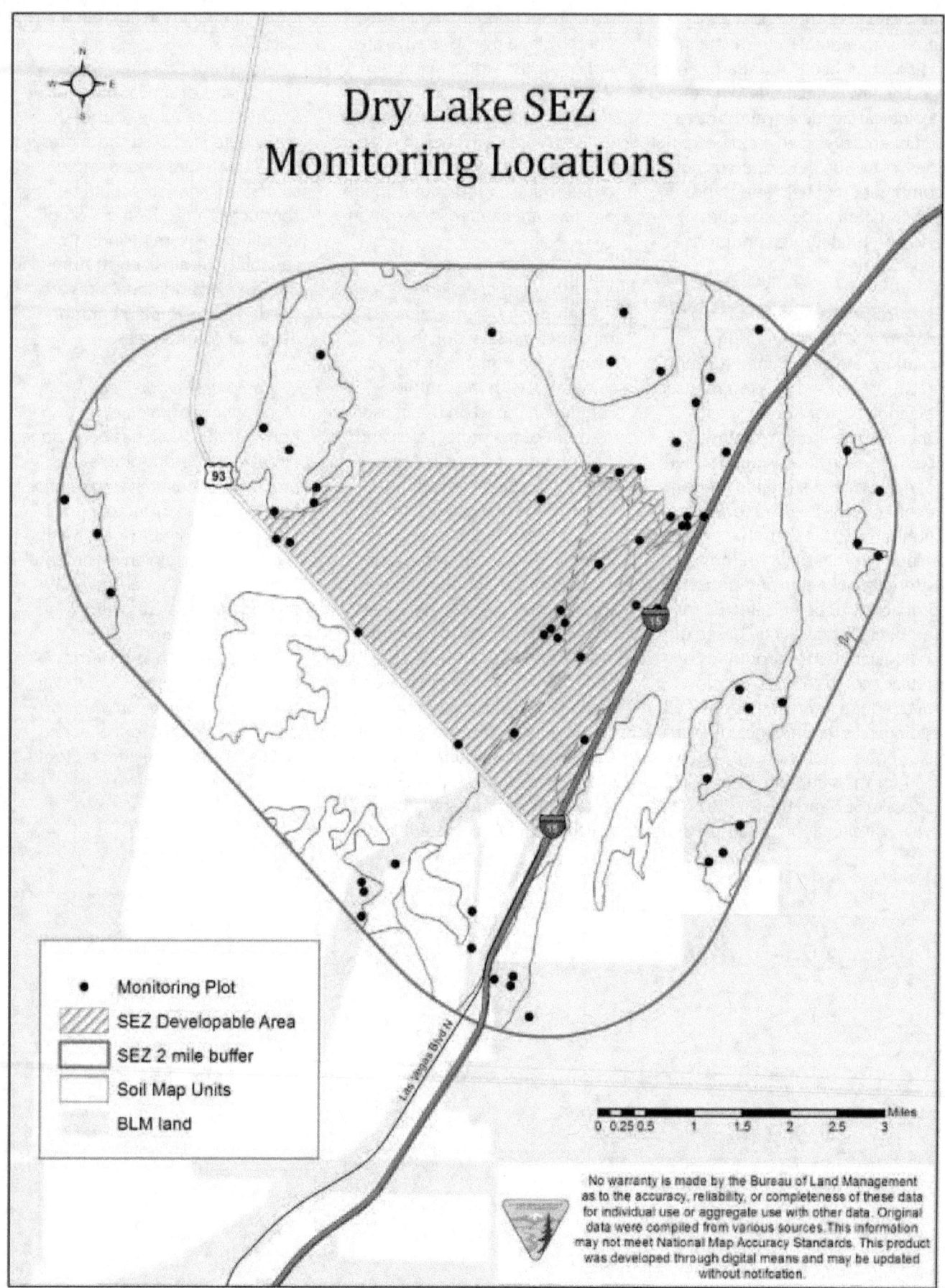

Figure 2-11. Example of a stratified, nonbiased sampling schema for the Dry Lake Solar Energy Zone.

Remote sensing technologies provide several benefits. They support the collection of spatially comprehensive datasets that are not otherwise readily available. In addition, the collection of data from a satellite or aircraft is nonintrusive, a very valuable feature for assessing ecologically and culturally sensitive areas. Semiautomated data processing of remotely sensed images can be a cost-effective way to reliably detect and identify features and quantify parameters over large areas more frequently. This feature is desirable for monitoring spatially heterogeneous and temporally dynamic arid and semiarid environments. Historic archives of remotely sensed data permit retrospective assessments and are thus suitable for long-term monitoring (Washington-Allen et al. 2006).

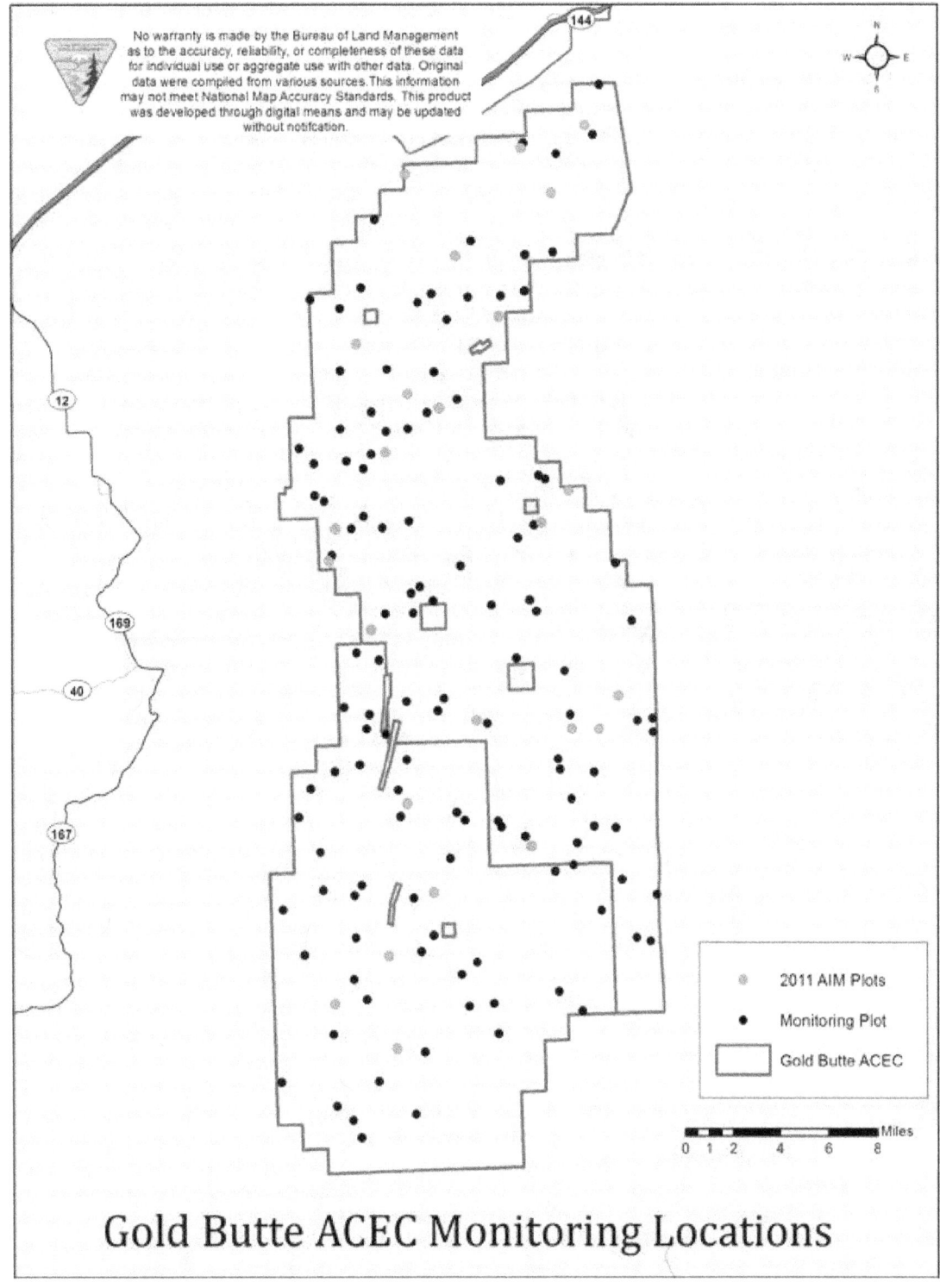

Gold Butte ACEC Monitoring Locations

Figure 2-12. Example of a stratified, nonbiased sampling schema for the Gold Butte Area of Critical Environmental Concern.

The limitations of remote sensing are that such measurements are indirect, and the spatial sampling unit (i.e., pixel) is arbitrary. In remote sensing, spectral reflectance signals from elements on the ground are assumed to be isolated from environmental and instrumental noise (Stow 1995). Further, targets are assumed to be spectrally separable from background, and different target types are assumed to have unique spectral signatures (Friedl, McGwire, and McIver 2001). The BLM interdisciplinary team should consult the AIM Strategy guidance and remote sensing experts to investigate cost-effective ways to incorporate the use of remote sensing technologies into the monitoring of mitigation actions.

Step 4. Develop Analysis and Reporting System.

Interpreting the data to determine the status, departure, or rate of change requires comparison of data collected via field sampling and/or remote sensing against indicators of ecological attributes for reference conditions. These reference conditions will be based on site or landscape potential which is described in ecological site descriptions. Ecological sites are the basis for the monitoring schema because they react similarly to factors like disturbance or degradation (historic or current), which can lead to alternative stable plant communities outside the historic potential of the site. For this reason, ecological sites are a basic unit for analysis and reporting. Elements of an ecological site description that are helpful for defining reference conditions and interpreting departure from reference conditions include: state-and-transition conceptual models of plant community changes in response to disturbance or management; descriptions of the range of plant communities that could exist on the site in addition to the potential vegetation; descriptions of anthropogenic and natural disturbances and their potential to cause changes in plant communities; descriptions of dynamic soil properties (e.g., organic matter content, soil aggregate stability); and amount of bare ground.

Step 5. Define Adaptive Management Approach.

The BLM will use information derived from the Dry Lake monitoring plan to determine if resource management objectives described in the Las Vegas RMP— the Dry Lake SEZ, the 2-mile buffer zone around the Dry Lake SEZ, and the areas where regional mitigation actions will occur—are being met. If the objectives are not being met, the monitoring program information will be used to make necessary management adjustments to the mitigation actions. Reporting at multiple scales will inform decisionmakers on the effectiveness of management and mitigation actions, opportunities for adaptive management (e.g., adjusting operational parameters, modifying mitigation actions, and/or adding new mitigation actions), refinement of conceptual models, and evaluation of the monitoring program itself. Adaptive changes will be subject to environmental analysis, land use planning, and public involvement, as appropriate.

2.10 Implementation Strategy

This project considered impacts that are likely to occur with the full build-out of the Dry Lake SEZ identified in the Final Solar PEIS. The project team found that while the potential for avoiding and/or mitigating many of the impacts onsite is good, the following impacts are likely to be unavoidable:

- The loss of desert tortoise habitat and the potential loss of individual desert tortoises. The desert tortoise is listed as a threatened species under the Endangered Species Act.

- The loss of habitat and the potential loss of individual animals for the following BLM special status species: Gila monster, Mojave Desert sidewinder, ferruginous hawk, golden eagle, loggerhead shrike, and Le Conte's thrasher.

- The loss of rosy two-toned penstemon habitat and the potential loss of individual plants. The rosy two-toned penstemon is a BLM special status species plant.

- The loss of ecosystem services and the human uses depending on them, as a result of development and until the lease expires and the site is restored. The primary components of an ecological system are: soils, vegetation, water, air, and wildlife.

- The visual impacts that will occur will exceed allowable levels in an area designated as VRM Class II in the Las Vegas RMP (BLM 1998).

In addition, the following unavoidable impacts were identified as having the potential to occur, depending on the way the area is developed, the success of onsite mitigation activities, data gaps, and/or the discovery of unanticipated resources:

- Introduction and spread of invasive/noxious weeds.

- Alterations to surface hydrology.

- Loss of cultural resources.

- Increased density of desert tortoise in the Coyote Springs ACEC (which was established for tortoise recovery).

- Visual resources as seen from nearby specially designated areas.

- Certain Native American concerns (e.g., loss of habitat and spiritual values).

Accordingly, and consistent with the management prescriptions for the affected resources in the Las Vegas RMP, the project team recommends the following regional mitigation goals:

- Sustain the populations of federally listed species so they no longer need protection under the Endangered Species Act.

- Manage habitats for nonlisted special status species to support viable populations so future listing is not necessary.

- Mitigate the loss of plants and habitat for the rosy two-toned penstemon to support viable populations in which the SEZ is located so that future listing is not necessary.

- Restore and/or protect the creosote-bursage vegetation community disrupted by development (taking into account the existing landscape condition in the SEZ).

- Restore and/or protect the visual resource values altered by development of the SEZ (taking into account the existing condition of visual resource values in the Dry Lake SEZ).

To achieve these goals, the project team recommends mitigation actions be undertaken in the Gold Butte ACEC. The Gold Butte ACEC was established in the Las Vegas RMP (BLM 1998). It has an area of approximately 350,000 acres (1416 km^2). The primary resource values listed in the RMP are:

- Cultural and historic resources.
- Scenic values.
- Wildlife habitat.
- Special status species habitat.
- Botanical resources.

The Gold Butte ACEC was selected from several potential regional mitigation candidate locations for the following reasons:

- The Mojave Basin and Range REA (NatureServe 2013) suggests that creosote-bursage vegetation in the Gold Butte ACEC may persist longer under climate change than the other nominated ACECs.

- Niche modeling, completed by the National Park Service for the Lake Mead National Recreation Area, suggests, under future climate change, high-quality desert tortoise habitat will remain in the Gold Butte ACEC while most of the adjacent desert tortoise habitat in the national recreation area will decline and disappear.

- Road decommissioning and restoration is proposed as a Dry Lake SEZ regional mitigation activity. The Gold Butte ACEC has already completed road designations. Road designations have not been completed on the other ACECs.

- Reseeding burn scars is proposed as a Dry Lake SEZ regional mitigation activity. The Gold Butte ACEC suffered multiple wildfires in 2005 and 2006 and could benefit from restoration. The other ACECs have had fewer fires.

- The Gold Butte ACEC is an important landscape corridor between Lake Mead and the Virgin Mountains for game species managed by the Nevada Department of Wildlife.

The recommended regional mitigation actions are as follows:

1. Prevent further degradation of the ACEC, and ensure the durability of the conservation investment by:

   a. Augmenting BLM law enforcement capacity sufficient to maintain ranger patrols in the ACEC.
   b. Providing a monitor to track activities in and impacts to the ACEC.
   c. Building the capacity to respond in a timely manner to activities that threaten resource values.
   d. Providing treatment for noxious weeds and maintaining fuel breaks to protect the area.

2. Restore creosote-bursage vegetation on closed roads, burn scars, and other anthropogenic impacts. Included in this goal is the procurement of genetically appropriate native seed to complete these restoration activities.

Any authorized mitigation activities will likely occur over a 30-year period, the expected lifetime of a solar facility lease in the Dry Lake SEZ. This extended time period is critical for implementation and to provide durability. Vegetation management in the Mojave Desert takes time; the conditions for seed germination and establishment typically occur once every 8 to 10 years. It takes time to develop the capacity to build and maintain a restoration program; it can take up to 5 years to collect or procure the genetically appropriate native seed needed for restoration and rehabilitation. By implementing the mitigation over 30 years, funds can be used to prudently respond to current and future needs. The proposed mitigation location

and actions will allow the BLM to provide for sustainable use by the public and conservation that will benefit future generations.

All of the recommended actions and the location are consistent with the current Las Vegas RMP. The Las Vegas RMP is currently being revised. It is recommended that the team developing the RMP revision consider incorporating a regional-level strategy for mitigating the unavoidable and cumulative impacts that may occur as a result of land use authorizations executed under the revised RMP.

In order to increase the probability of success in achieving and maintaining the mitigation goals and to facilitate effective adaptive management (including action to protect the resources identified as having the potential to be impacted), the project team recommends the development and implementation of a monitoring and adaptive management plan.

In order to fund the recommended mitigation actions, monitoring, and adaptive management, the project team recommends a regional mitigation fee be assessed to the developer(s) similar to the example provided in Section 2.6. This fee will be in addition to the Endangered Species Act Section 7 fee (currently $824/acre). It is recommended that a third-party entity be retained to manage mitigation funds.

The findings and recommendations offered here are intended to inform the decisionmaking process associated with leasing land in the Dry Lake SEZ for utility-scale solar development. At the discretion of the BLM authorized officer, all or part of these recommendations could be included in the decisionmaking process.

References

BLM (Bureau of Land Management). 1998. Proposed Las Vegas Resource Management Plan and Final Environmental Impact Statement. Bureau of Land Management, Las Vegas Field Office, Las Vegas, NV.

BLM (Bureau of Land Management). 2012. Approved Resource Management Plan Amendments/Record of Decision (ROD) for Solar Energy Development in Six Southwestern States. Bureau of Land Management.

BLM (Bureau of Land Management). 2013a. Best Management Practices for Reducing Visual Impacts of Renewable Energy Facilities on BLM-Administered Lands. Bureau of Land Management, Cheyenne, WY.

BLM (Bureau of Land Management). 2013b. Interim Policy, Draft – "Regional Mitigation" Manual Section – 1794. Instruction Memorandum No. 2013-142. Bureau of Land Management, Washington, DC.

BLM (Bureau of Land Management). Forthcoming. Procedural Guidance for Developing Solar Regional Mitigation Strategies. Bureau of Land Management, Washington Office, Washington, DC.

BLM and DOE (Bureau of Land Management and U.S. Department of Energy). 2012. Final Programmatic Environmental Impact Statement (PEIS) for Solar Energy Development in Six Southwestern States. FES 12-24, DOE/EIS-0403. Bureau of Land Management and U.S. Department of Energy.

Brussard, P.F., K.H. Berry, M.E. Gilpin, E.R. Jacobson, D.J. Morafke, C.R. Schwalbe, C.R. Tracy, and F.C. Vasek. 1994. Desert Tortoise (Mojave Population) Recovery Plan. U.S. Fish and Wildlife Service, Portland, OR.

Elzinga, C.L., D.W. Salzer, and J.W. Willoughby. 1998. Measuring and Monitoring Plant Populations. Tech Ref 1730-1. Bureau of Land Management, National Business Center, Denver, CO. http://www.blm.gov/nstc/library/pdf/MeasAndMon.pdf.

Friedl, M.A., K.C. McGwire, and D.K. McIver. 2001. An Overview of Uncertainty in Optical Remotely Sensed Data for Ecological Applications. p. 258-283. In: C.T. Hunsaker, M.F. Goodchild, M.A. Friedl, and T.J. Case (eds). Spatial Uncertainty in Ecology: Implications for Remote Sensing and GIS Applications, Springer, NY.

Hamilton, M.E., and S.R. Kokos. 2011. Clark County Rare Plant Habitat Modeling. Environmental Planning Group, Inc., and Bureau of Reclamation. http://bit.ly/Qbm19H.

MacKinnon, W.C., J.W. Karl, G.R. Toevs, J.J. Taylor, M. Karl, C.S. Spurrier, and J.E. Herrick. 2011. BLM Core Terrestrial Indicators and Methods. Tech Note 440. Bureau of Land Management, National Operations Center, Denver, CO.

NatureServe. 2013. Mojave Basin and Range Rapid Ecoregional Assessment. http://www.blm.gov/wo/st/en/prog/more/Landscape_Approach/reas/mojave.html#memo.

Pellant, M., P. Shaver, D.A. Pyke, and J.E. Herrick. 2005. Interpreting Indicators of Rangeland Health, Version 4. Tech Ref 1734-6. Bureau of Land Management, National Science and Technology Center, Denver, CO. http://www.blm.gov/nstc/library/techref.htm.

SWCA and University of Arizona (SWCA Environmental Consultants and Bureau of Applied Research in Anthropology). 2011. Ethnographic and Class I Records Searches for Proposed Solar Energy Zones in California, Nevada, and Utah for the Bureau of Land Management's Solar Programmatic Environmental Impact Statement. SWCA Project No. 16983. SWCA Environmental Consultants and University of Arizona, Albuquerque, NM.

Stow, D.A. 2005. Monitoring Ecosystem Response to Global Change: Multitemporal Remote Sensing Analysis. p. 254-286. In: J.M. Moreno et al. (eds). Global Change and Mediterranean-Type Ecosystems. Springer-Verlag New York, Inc.

Toevs, G.R., J.J. Taylor, C.S. Spurrier, W.C. MacKinnon, and M.R. Bobo. 2011. Assessment, Inventory, and Monitoring Strategy for Integrated Renewable Resources Management. Bureau of Land Management, National Operations Center, Denver, CO.

Washington-Allen, R.A., N.E. West, R.D. Ramsey, and R.A. Efroymson. 2006. A Protocol for Retrospective Remote Sensing-Based Ecological Monitoring of Rangelands. Rangeland Ecology and Management 59 (1): 19-29.

Appendix A:

Impact Assessment Summary Table

The following table summarizes the Bureau of Land Management and Argonne National Laboratory subject matter expert responses to the process steps and criteria used to identify the unavoidable impacts that are likely to occur as a result of solar development in the Dry Lake Solar Energy Zone. The process steps and criteria for identifying unavoidable impacts are outlined in Section 2.4.3.1 of this document.

Dry Lake Solar Energy Zone: Potential Unavoidable Impact Summary

Resource/ Issue	Are impacts compre-hensive and accurate?	Do impacts need to be amended?	Any additional design features?	To what degree are impacts likely to be mitigated onsite?	Are impacts likely to be adequately mitigated?	Justification for impacts being or not being mitigated onsite:
Soils/Erosion	Yes	No	No	Little can be done onsite to mitigate the loss of up to 5,717 acres of soil. Avoidance (not developing some areas) will reduce the acreage, and soil stabilization measures can reduce soil erosion post disturbance.	No	The degree of disturbance required will result in the loss of a significant quantity of biological soils. While predicted recovery rates for biologi-cal soil crusts vary from study to study, most put the recovery rate for damaged crust between 20 to 250 years, once disturbance is removed. For desert pavement, natural recovery rates are in the millennia, and large-scale disturbances are not thought to be recoverable.
Wildlife	Yes	No	No	Little can be done onsite to mitigate the loss of up to 5,717 acres of general wildlife habitat. Avoidance (such as not developing riparian areas or under existing power lines) will reduce the acreage.	No	Development of the Dry Lake SEZ will likely impact up to 5,717 acres of wildlife habitat.
Special Status Species - Animals	Yes (The PEIS list of species potentially occurring in the SEZ has been mod-ified on the basis of BLM local data; predisturbance surveys to con-firm absence of species potentially present but not further evaluated under the SRMP may be required of developers. If found, the need for regional mitigation of impacts to those species would be addressed at that time.)	No	No	Onsite mitigation will reduce, but will not eliminate, the loss of special status animal species and their habitat. Development of the Dry Lake SEZ would result in loss of individuals and/or habitat of six special status animal species (listed in the far right column) as well as the federally threatened desert tortoise and migratory bird species protected under the Migratory Bird Treaty Act. Since birds are highly mobile, they will most likely move out of harm's way during construction, except during breeding season. Effects to individual migratory birds and bird nests can be avoided by not constructing during the breeding season (March 1- August 31). If construc-tion takes place during the breeding season, nest surveys will be conducted. If bird nests are found, then an appropriately sized buffer will be placed around the nest. No construction will be allowed within the buffer, until the birds have fledged. Although individual golden eagles and their nests will not be directly affected, construction will affect golden eagle foraging habitat. Reptiles tend to take shelter in burrows and do not move out of harm's way. Individual reptiles can be killed or maimed during construction. Desert tortoise minimization measures include: translocation/relocation, project fencing, education programs, perch deterrents, trash program, authorized biologists/monitors onsite during construction, clearance surveys, educational signs, minimizing ground disturbance, no pooling of water (dust control), and covering holes and trenches when not in use.	No	Six BLM sensitive species are known to occur or likely to occur in the SEZ (Gila monster, Mojave Desert sidewinder, ferruginous hawk, golden eagle, loggerhead shrike, and Le Conte's thrash-er), as well as the federally threatened desert tortoise and migratory bird species protected under the Migratory Bird Treaty Act. All would suffer unavoidable impacts. Complete build-out of the Dry Lake SEZ would directly impact up to 5,717 acres. In the context of the National Environmental Policy Act, direct impacts on the overall range of these species would not be significant because the Dry Lake SEZ is only a small portion of the overall range (see Final PEIS for specific percentages). However, when combined with other BLM lands actions (including other renewable energy development projects, utility corridors and land disposal), multiple use activities (including mining and off-highway vehicle recreation), and threats (fragmentation, increased competition with invasive species), development of the Dry Lake SEZ could cause continued population declines of the above mentioned species.

Resource/ Issue	Are impacts comprehensive and accurate?	Do impacts need to be amended?	Any additional design features?	To what degree are impacts likely to be mitigated onsite?	Are impacts likely to be adequately mitigated?	Justification for impacts being or not being mitigated onsite:
Vegetation	Yes	No	No	Little can be done onsite to mitigate the loss of up to 5,717 acres of vegetation. While the native vegetation on a small portion of the disturbed areas could be restored, the Mojave Desert is extremely slow to recover from disturbance. Estimates suggest that, without active restoration, it takes the Mojave Desert 76 years for reestablishment of perennial plant cover and 215 years for reestablishment of both perennial and annual species cover. This means the cumulative impacts of ground-disturbing activities are additive over time. It also means the BLM can use restoration as a way to mitigate cumulative impacts because restoration can speed up recovery time.	No	Development of the Dry Lake SEZ would result in the direct loss of up to 5,717 acres of Mojave creosote-bursage scrub, saltbush scrub, and mesquite-acacia woodland. These native plant communities, along with the intact biological soil crusts and desert pavement within them, provide ecosystem services including: stabilizing soils against wind and water erosion; maintaining air and water quality; maintaining nutrient cycling; maintaining landscape connectivity including the dispersal and migration of species across the landscape; protecting against colonization by nonnative weeds and protecting against wildfire; and providing shelter and forage for game species, migratory birds, six BLM special status animal species, and general wildlife species. Development would result in direct removal or disturbance of these native plant communities, special soil environments, and the ecosystem services they provide. The direct impacts would probably not be significant in the sense of NEPA; however, on a larger scale the cumulative loss of these services could cost the public in terms of reduced environmental quality and cost BLM funding if it becomes necessary to implement management actions to compensate for their disruption or loss.
Special Status Species - Vegetation	Yes	Yes[1]	No	Little can be done onsite to mitigate the loss of the one special status plant species known to exist in the Dry Lake SEZ. Development of the Dry Lake SEZ would result in the removal of rosy two-toned penstemon plants and the alteration of 5,717 acres of habitat. Given low population densities and dispersed distribution of the species across the SEZ, avoidance of individual plants is not practical and would excessively fragment the remaining population.	No	One BLM special status plant species, the rosy two-toned penstemon (*Penstemon bicolor ssp. roseus*) would suffer unavoidable impacts.
Visual Resources	Yes	No	Yes (managed development plan for the SEZ; coordination with City of North Las Vegas planners).	Part of the SEZ is currently managed as VRM Class III under the applicable BLM land use plan. Onsite mitigation will reduce, but will not eliminate, visual impacts to scenic values. The Final Solar PEIS identified moderate to strong visual contrasts in the following specially designated areas in the vicinity of the SEZ: Desert National Wildlife Refuge, Old Spanish National Historic Trail, Arrow Canyon Wilderness, Muddy Mountains Wilderness, and Nellis Dunes Special Recreation Management Area. Potential impact on night skies. Implementing design features, such as selecting paint colors that blend with the environment, minimizing vegetation removal, and using good lighting design and operating procedures, can reduce contrast.	No	Development of the Dry Lake SEZ would introduce changes in visual forms, lines, colors, and textures that would contrast strongly with the surrounding landscape in the SEZ, and because of the large size of the facilities and their highly reflective surfaces, the Dry Lake SEZ could be visible for long distances from surrounding lands. The SEZ is a flat area devoid of tall vegetation, and consequently, solar facilities within the SEZ generally could not be screened from view from nearby lands. While onsite mitigation would reduce visual contrasts caused by solar facilities within the SEZ, it would not likely reduce impacts to less than moderate or strong levels for nearby viewers.

Resource/ Issue	Are impacts comprehensive and accurate?	Do impacts need to be amended?	Any additional design features?	To what degree are impacts likely to be mitigated onsite?	Are impacts likely to be adequately mitigated?	Justification for impacts being or not being mitigated onsite:
Specially Designated Areas	Yes	No	No	See the Hydrology section in this table. The Final Solar PEIS identified moderate to strong visual contrasts in the following specially designated areas in the vicinity of the SEZ: Desert National Wildlife Refuge, Old Spanish National Historic Trail, Arrow Canyon Wilderness, Muddy Mountains Wilderness, and Nellis Dunes Special Recreation Management Area.	Maybe for Coyote Springs ACEC but not for visual impacts at other specially designated areas.	It depends if impacts on hydrology extend to the Coyote Springs ACEC. For visual impacts, full development of the SEZ with solar facilities would cause moderate to strong visual contrasts that could not be hidden from view from the specially designated areas.
Military	Yes	No	No	The Air Force has stated that glare, thermal effects, structure height greater than 250 ft, lighting of structures, and transmission lines could adversely affect operations. Collision hazards can be reduced by restricting maximum development height. While the probability of flight crews parachuting into the area as a result of in-flight emergencies is low, the safety hazard posed by solar facilities cannot be completely mitigated onsite.	No	Because the development area is under the approach and departure routes for military aircraft traveling between Nellis Air Force Base and the Nevada Test and Training Range, there is a heightened risk of emergencies occurring as aircraft pass over the site. Such emergencies can involve the jettisoning of ordnance, crews ejecting and parachuting, and aircraft crashing. Restriction on project height can reduce collision hazards.
Native American Concerns	Yes	No	No	See Hydrology and Wildlife sections in this table.	No	Tribal representatives have identified impacts on hydrology and wildlife as concerns. The extent of the impacts on hydrology depends on the technology and on the cumulative use of water resources. Unavoidable impacts on wildlife habitat are expected. Loss of wildlife habitat can be mitigated to some extent onsite.
Invasive/ Noxious Weeds	Yes	No	No	The active and prolonged implementation of design features can greatly reduce, but not eliminate, the risk of the establishment and spread of invasive species.	Maybe	Onsite mitigation will reduce, but will not eliminate, the potential for invasive species. The degree of disturbance creates a significant opportunity for the establishment of invasive species and weeds.
Hydrology (Water/ Watershed/ Water Quality)	Yes	No	No	While it depends on the water demands of the development and whether the subsurface hydrology is affected, some impacts might be mitigated by the migration of water used for dust suppression and/or for cleaning mirrors back into the ground.	Maybe	The nature of the solar technology deployed will dictate water requirements. Onsite mitigation will reduce, but will not eliminate, the need for water. While the groundwater in the hydrologic basin is overallocated, it is currently not overused. If all allocations are fully used, the water used in solar operations, in conjunction with water used outside the SEZ, would contribute to a decline in the water table.
Riparian	Yes	No	No	Most impacts can be mitigated onsite by avoiding development in the washes and by the installation of engineering controls on surface water runoff/ erosion. The riparian areas that occur within the SEZ are shallow ephemeral washes and have been excluded from the developable area.	Maybe	It depends on the engineering controls. Development may alter ephemeral stream channels that can impact flooding and debris flows during storms, groundwater recharge, ecological habitats, and riparian vegetation communities. Reductions to the connectivity of these areas with existing surface waters and groundwater could limit water availability and thus alter the ability of the area to support vegetation and aquatic species. This could reduce overall stability of the natural landscape.
Cultural	Yes	No	No	A preconstruction cultural survey and the programmatic agreement establishing a protocol for treating cultural resources if they are discovered during construction decrease the risk of disturbing or destroying cultural resources. The eligible Old Spanish Trail/Mormon Road linear feature can be avoided.	Maybe	The discovery of new cultural sites is always a possibility, and adequate mitigation would be dependent on the resources discovered and their relative significance in the region.

Resource/ Issue	Are impacts compre-hensive and accurate?	Do impacts need to be amended?	Any additional design features?	To what degree are impacts likely to be mitigated onsite?	Are impacts likely to be adequately mitigated?	Justification for impacts being or not being mitigated onsite:
Acoustics	Yes	No	No	Some temporary acoustic impacts are expected during construction. Onsite standards and monitor-ing are expected to keep impacts in an acceptable range.	Yes	The area is currently impacted by traffic noise from Interstate15 and Route 93 and the railroad adjacent to the site. Additional impacts from solar development are expected to be tempo-rary, localized, and neither significantly louder than or out of character with current noise.
Air Quality	Yes	No	No	Some temporary impacts are expected during construction, primarily from construction vehicle emissions and from dust kicked up by construction vehicles and by wind blowing over disturbed crust. Onsite mitigation, such as dust suppression, and monitoring are expected to keep impacts in an acceptable range (less than the National Ambient Air Quality Standards for carbon monoxide and particulate matter).	Yes	The area is currently impacted by emission from vehicles traveling on Interstate15 and Route 93, the Apex landfill, the mines and mills operating on the south end of the SEZ, and the natural gas-fired power plants operating on and around the SEZ. Additional impacts are ex-pected to be temporary and are not expected to result in noncompliance with National Ambient Air Quality Standards.
Environmen-tal Justice	Yes	No	No	No adverse impacts are anticipated.	Yes	While there are minority and/or low income populations within 50 miles, they are more than 10 miles away, and views of the SEZ are restricted.
Fire	Yes	No	No	Onsite mitigation can significantly reduce the chanc-es of a wildfire. Historically, the SEZ has seen very little fire disturbance. However, this may increase if burnable vegetation becomes established. Miti-gation that reduces the establishment of burnable invasive species will maintain a low risk status. Onsite mitigation would include a requirement for the development and implementation of a fire safety and emergency response plan, including fuel inventory, to be developed and executed during con-struction and operations, including fire/fuel breaks and design features to help minimize risk.	Yes	The area is low fire risk to begin with. This would change only if burnable invasive species were allowed to establish.
Hazardous Waste	Yes	No	No	Virtually all impacts can be mitigated onsite. The design features, which require development of an emergency response plan, will reduce the chances of a hazardous material release and provide a protocol for mitigating the site, should one occur.	Yes	The implementation of design features for handling any hazardous substances will reduce the risk of exposure and/or release and, should one occur, specify the emergency procedures for protecting public safety and for remediating the site.
Lands and Realty	Yes	No	No	Virtually all impacts can be mitigated onsite. Ac-cording to regulation, any and all solar development must occur in deference to all previously existing rights. In addition, the BLM Southern Nevada District Office has made the decision to remove from leasing the areas within the SEZ encumbered by existing rights-of-way (plus a 200-foot buffer).	Yes	By regulation, any new activity must occur in deference to existing rights. Thus, potential impacts have been avoided.
Minerals	Yes	No	No	Virtually all impacts can be mitigated onsite by avoiding existing mining and mill site claims. The Southern Nevada District Office has made the decision to remove from leasing the existing mining and mill site claims.	Yes	By regulation, any new activity must occur in deference to existing rights. Thus, potential impacts have been avoided.
Paleonto-logical	Yes	No	No	No mitigation is required as no paleontological resources are known or are expected to exist in the SEZ. Design features will reduce the risk that any paleontological resources that are discovered will be destroyed.	Yes	Not applicable—there are no known paleon-tological resources on site, and the geology suggests the potential is low.
Livestock Grazing	Yes	No	No	No mitigation is necessary as there are no impacts.	Yes	Not applicable—there are no grazing allot-ments within the SEZ.

Resource/ Issue	Are impacts compre-hensive and accurate?	Do impacts need to be amended?	Any additional design features?	To what degree are impacts likely to be mitigated onsite?	Are impacts likely to be adequately mitigated?	Justification for impacts being or not being mitigated onsite:
Recreation (Includes Travel Man-agement Areas)	Yes	No	No	Virtually all impacts on recreation can be mitigated onsite. The potential impacts are primarily related to providing access to Dry Lake and the Arrow Canyon mountain range to the west of the SEZ. Through a combination of avoidance, design features, and the establishment of alternative access routes to these areas, the potential impacts can be adequately mitigated onsite.	Yes	Relatively little recreation currently occurs in the SEZ. Access to the Arrow Canyon Range and Dry Lake can be maintained by existing and/ or new routes. If new routes are established, a NEPA analysis would be required for those routes.
Socioeco-nomic	Yes	No	No	Possible adverse impacts of in-migrating workers required for project construction and operation (e.g., hiring of police, fire fighters, and teachers and pro-viding services to new area workers and families). Onsite mitigation could include requiring developers to secure agreements for local government services as a condition of a "Notice to Proceed."	Yes	Any adverse impacts caused by the requirement for local government services would be miti-gated by the requirement for the developer to secure agreements as a condition of the "Notice to Proceed."
Transporta-tion	Yes	No	No	Virtually all impacts on transportation can be mitigated onsite. The potential impacts are primarily related to providing access to Dry Lake and the Arrow Canyon Range to the west of the SEZ. Through a combination of avoidance, design features, and the establishment of alternative access routes to these areas, the potential impacts can be adequately mitigated onsite.	Yes	Relatively few transportation routes would be impacted by development in the SEZ. Alterna-tive routes to the Arrow Canyon Range and Dry Lake can be established.
Wild Horses and Burros	Yes	No	No	No mitigation is necessary as the SEZ is not part of a herd management area, and no horses or burros are known to exist in the area.	Yes	The SEZ is not part of a herd management area, and no horses or burros are known to exist in the area.
Wilderness and Lands with Wilderness Character-istics	Yes	No	No	No mitigation is necessary as there are no desig-nated wilderness areas or lands with wilderness characteristics within or adjacent to the SEZ. Be-cause of extensive existing development within the SEZ (roads, power lines, pipelines, active mill-site, electrical substation, and natural gas-fired power plant), the area lacks wilderness characteristics.	Yes	Not applicable—resources would not be impacted.

[1] The Final Solar PEIS identified seven BLM-Nevada special status plants that occur in and around the Dry Lake SEZ. However, only the rosy two-toned penstemon is expected to occur in the Dry Lake SEZ. To determine potential impacts on BLM special status plants, the BLM reviewed occurrence data and "Clark County Rare Plant Habitat Modeling" (Hamilton and Kokos 2011). The habitat modeling report can be downloaded from the Clark County Desert Conservation Program website at http://bit.ly/Qbm19H.

Appendix B:

Regional and Dry Lake Solar Energy Zone Conceptual Models

Conceptual models are used to understand ecosystem interactions at an ecoregional scale (Tier 1), the solar development scale (Tier 2), and the SEZ-specific scale (Tier 3). The models used for the pilot Dry Lake Solar Energy Zone Solar Regional Mitigation Planning Project (as revised with stakeholder input) are presented here. Additional, more complex models may be constructed if needed to support impact assessment in the future.

Tier 1 Conceptual Model, Mojave Basin and Range Ecoregion Model

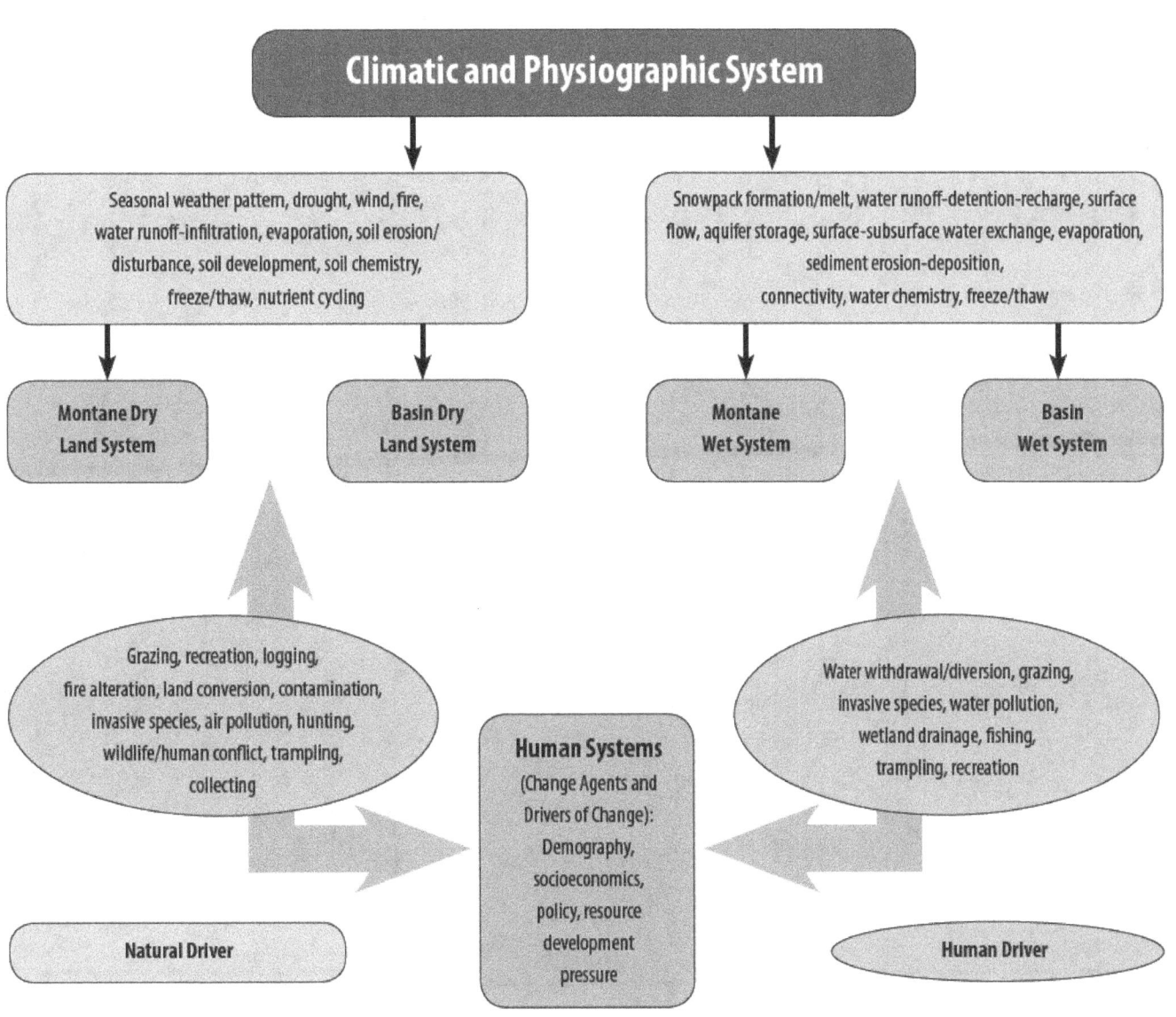

Tier 2 Conceptual Model, Resource-Based Model

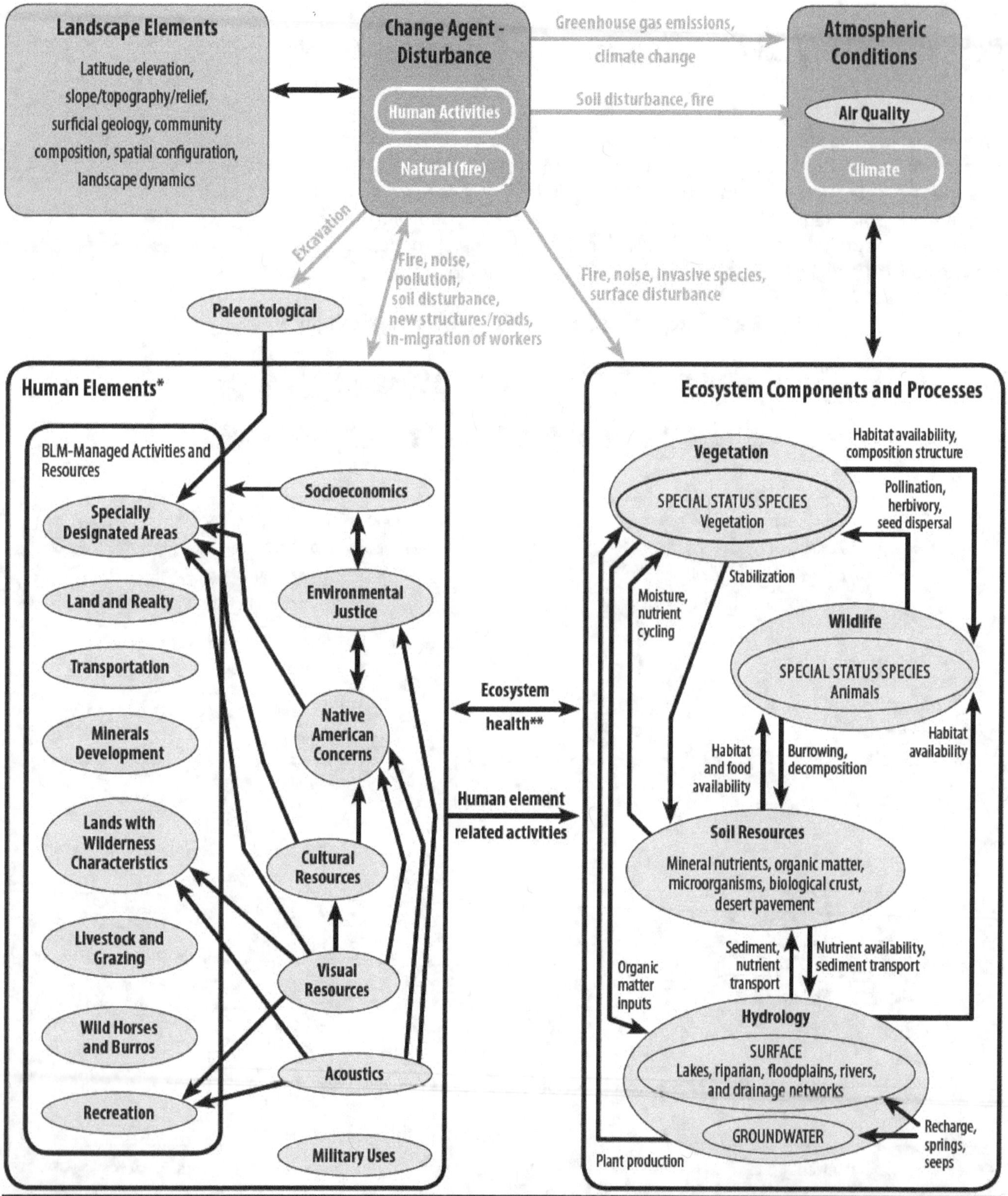

Landscape Elements

Latitude, elevation, slope/topography/relief, surficial geology, community composition, spatial configuration, landscape dynamics

Change Agent - Disturbance

Human Activities

Natural (fire)

Greenhouse gas emissions, climate change

Soil disturbance, fire

Atmospheric Conditions

Air Quality

Climate

Excavation

Fire, noise, pollution, soil disturbance, new structures/roads, in-migration of workers

Fire, noise, invasive species, surface disturbance

Paleontological

Human Elements*

BLM-Managed Activities and Resources

Specially Designated Areas

Land and Realty

Transportation

Minerals Development

Lands with Wilderness Characteristics

Livestock and Grazing

Wild Horses and Burros

Recreation

Socioeconomics

Environmental Justice

Native American Concerns

Cultural Resources

Visual Resources

Acoustics

Military Uses

Ecosystem health**

Human element related activities

Ecosystem Components and Processes

Habitat availability, composition structure

Vegetation

SPECIAL STATUS SPECIES Vegetation

Pollination, herbivory, seed dispersal

Moisture, nutrient cycling

Stabilization

Wildlife

SPECIAL STATUS SPECIES Animals

Habitat availability

Habitat and food availability

Burrowing, decomposition

Soil Resources

Mineral nutrients, organic matter, microorganisms, biological crust, desert pavement

Organic matter inputs

Sediment, nutrient transport

Nutrient availability, sediment transport

Hydrology

SURFACE
Lakes, riparian, floodplains, rivers, and drainage networks

GROUNDWATER

Recharge, springs, seeps

Plant production

Legend

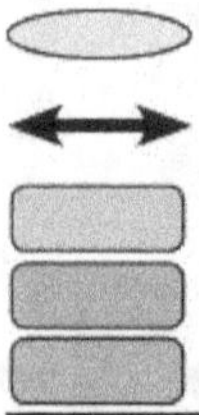

Resource and BLM-managed activities

Direction of processes (orange arrows associated with anthropogenic disturbance)

Natural drivers

Change agents

Atmospheric conditions

* Human elements include the human concerns and related resources for which impact evaluation was included in the Final Solar PEIS. These are activities and resources with (or requiring) human engagement in one of the following ways: (1) requires active participation in management of a resource or activity (e.g., lands and realty, specially designated areas, transportation, grazing, mineral development, recreation, military uses; (2) addresses the perspective or perception of a resource (e.g., visual resources, acoustics, lands with wilderness characteristics, cultural); and/or (3) addresses human-specific values (e.g., cultural resources, Native American concerns, socioeconomics, environmental justice).

** Ecosystem health is referred to as the degree to which the integrity of the soil and the ecological processes of the ecosystem are sustained (BLM Handbook H-4180-1). Ecosystem health can influence Native American concerns, visual resources, specially designated areas, and recreation. Human elements can also influence ecosystem components (e.g., recreation can compact soils, hunting can impact species, etc.).

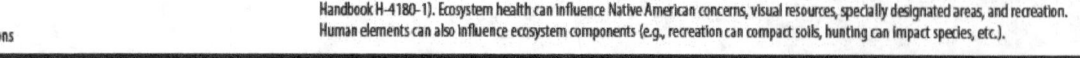

Tier 3 Conceptual Model, Dry Lake SEZ Solar Development Model

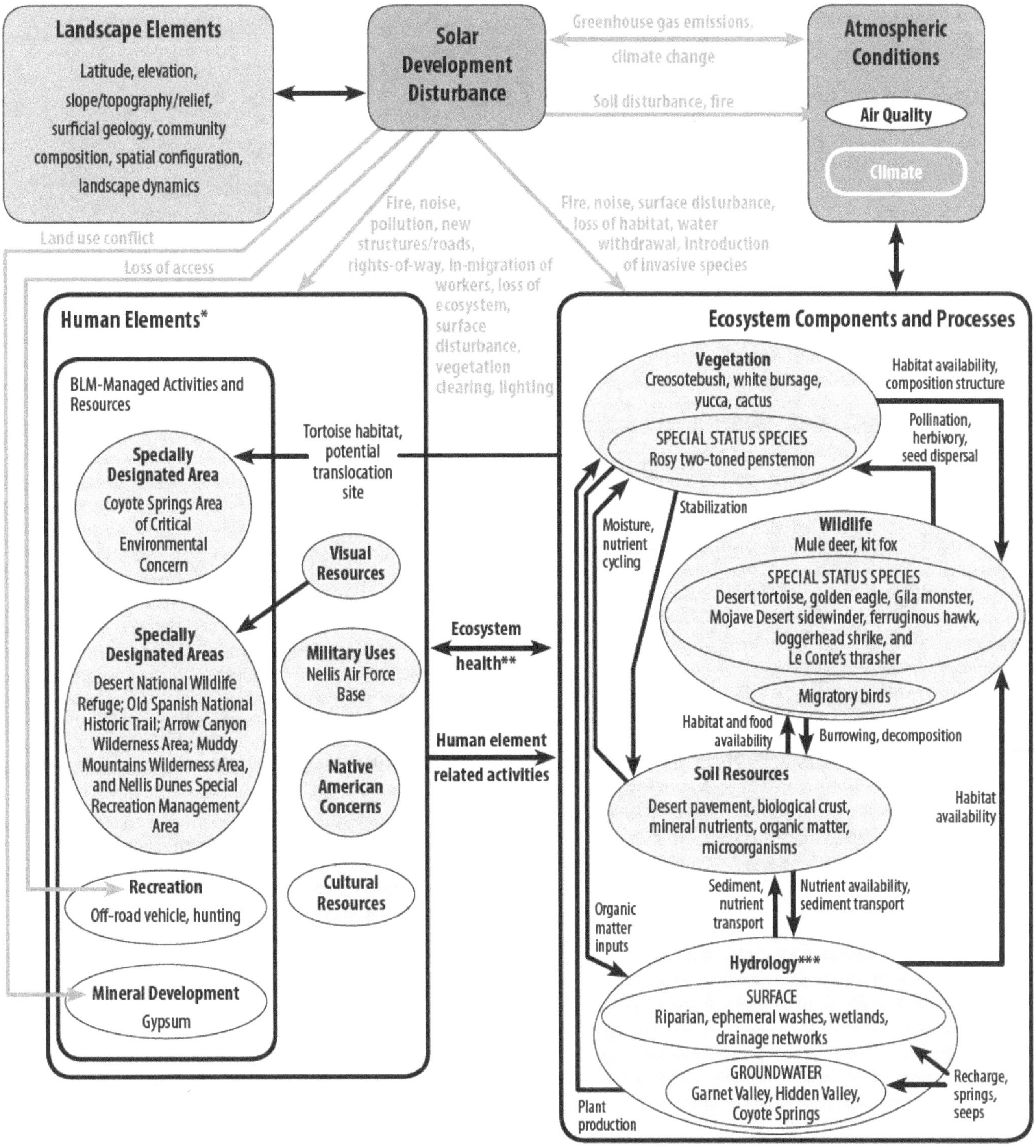

Landscape Elements

Latitude, elevation, slope/topography/relief, surficial geology, community composition, spatial configuration, landscape dynamics

Solar Development Disturbance

Greenhouse gas emissions, climate change

Soil disturbance, fire

Atmospheric Conditions

Air Quality

Climate

Land use conflict

Loss of access

Fire, noise, pollution, new structures/roads, rights-of-way, in-migration of workers, loss of ecosystem, surface disturbance, vegetation clearing, lighting

Fire, noise, surface disturbance, loss of habitat, water withdrawal, introduction of invasive species

Human Elements*

BLM-Managed Activities and Resources

Specially Designated Area
Coyote Springs Area of Critical Environmental Concern

Specially Designated Areas
Desert National Wildlife Refuge; Old Spanish National Historic Trail; Arrow Canyon Wilderness Area; Muddy Mountains Wilderness Area, and Nellis Dunes Special Recreation Management Area

Visual Resources

Military Uses
Nellis Air Force Base

Native American Concerns

Cultural Resources

Recreation
Off-road vehicle, hunting

Mineral Development
Gypsum

Tortoise habitat, potential translocation site

Ecosystem health**

Human element related activities

Ecosystem Components and Processes

Vegetation
Creosotebush, white bursage, yucca, cactus

SPECIAL STATUS SPECIES
Rosy two-toned penstemon

Habitat availability, composition structure

Pollination, herbivory, seed dispersal

Stabilization

Moisture, nutrient cycling

Wildlife
Mule deer, kit fox

SPECIAL STATUS SPECIES
Desert tortoise, golden eagle, Gila monster, Mojave Desert sidewinder, ferruginous hawk, loggerhead shrike, and Le Conte's thrasher

Migratory birds

Habitat and food availability

Burrowing, decomposition

Habitat availability

Soil Resources
Desert pavement, biological crust, mineral nutrients, organic matter, microorganisms

Sediment, nutrient transport

Nutrient availability, sediment transport

Organic matter inputs

Hydrology***

SURFACE
Riparian, ephemeral washes, wetlands, drainage networks

GROUNDWATER
Garnet Valley, Hidden Valley, Coyote Springs

Recharge, springs, seeps

Plant production

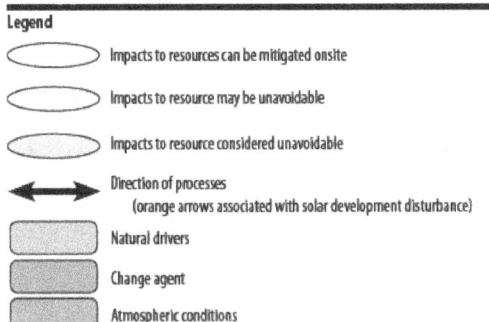

Legend

- Impacts to resources can be mitigated onsite
- Impacts to resource may be unavoidable
- Impacts to resource considered unavoidable
- Direction of processes (orange arrows associated with solar development disturbance)
- Natural drivers
- Change agent
- Atmospheric conditions

* Human elements include the human concerns and related resources for which impact evaluation was included in the Final Solar PEIS. These are activities and resources with (or requiring) human engagement in one of the following ways:
(1) requires active participation in management of a resource or activity (e.g., lands and realty, specially designated areas, transportation, grazing, mineral development, recreation, military uses; (2) addresses the perspective orperception f a resource (e.g., visual resources, acoustics, lands with wilderness characteristics, cultural); and/or (3) addresses human-specific values (e.g, cultural resources, Native American concerns, socioeconomics, environmental justice).

** Ecosystem health is referred to as the degree to which the integrity of the soil and the ecological processes of the ecosystem are sustained (BLM Handbook H-4180-1). Ecosystem health can influence Native American concerns, visual resources, specially designated areas, and recreation. Human elements can also influence ecosystem components (e.g., recreation can compact soils, hunting can impact species, etc.).

*** Unavoidable hydrologic impacts may occur due to changes in drainage and recharge patterns. Potential impacts to water availability will be mitigated onsite through the implementation of a net neutral use policy (water rights must be purchased).

Appendix C:

Summary Table: Impacts that May Warrant Regional Mitigation for the Dry Lake Solar Energy Zone[1]

Resource/ Issue	Unavoidable Impacts?[2]	How certain is it that the unavoidable impacts will occur?	How significant are the unavoidable impacts onsite?	How significant are the unavoidable impacts of developing the Dry Lake SEZ in the region (Mojave Desert)?[3]	Role in the ecosystem?[4]	Other considerations	Are potential unavoidable impacts likely to warrant regional mitigation?
Soils/ Erosion	Yes	Certain	Very—expect the total loss of biological soils and/or desert pavement over the entire developable area.	Trend: Decreasing. Approximately 8.8% of soil resources in the Mojave Desert have been altered by human development. For example, 3.8% of desert pavement in the Mojave Desert has been altered. A 0.2% increase in alteration of desert pavement is expected by 2025.	Basic component.	Natural regeneration of biological soils and/or desert pavement is very slow in the Mojave Desert.	Yes
Wildlife	Yes	Certain	Very—expect the loss of habitat for most general wildlife species over the entire developable area.	Trend: Decreasing. Approximately 7.1% of wildlife habitat in the Mojave Desert has been altered. A 1% increase in alteration is expected by 2025.	Basic component.		Yes—indirectly (as a component of the ecosystem).
Special Status Species - Animals	Yes	Loss of habitat is certain. Loss of animals is likely.	Very—expect the total loss of habitat for special status animal species over the entire developable area.	Trend: Decreasing. Habitat for special status species has been decreasing in the Mojave Desert; for example, 11.1% of habitat for desert tortoise has been altered at present, and an additional 1.4% is expected to be altered by 2025.	Basic component (along with other wildlife).	Mitigation of listed species is required by law and/or policy.	Yes
Vegetation	Yes	Certain	Very—expect the loss of all vegetation over the developable area of the SEZ, though mitigation may result in some remaining or replanted vegetation.	Trend: Decreasing. Approximately 7.1% of natural vegetation communities in the Mojave Desert have been altered by human development. A 1% increase in alteration is expected by 2025.	Basic component.	Natural regeneration of native vegetation is slow in the Mojave Desert.	Yes
Special Status Species - Vegetation	Yes	Loss of habitat is certain. Loss of plants is likely.	Very—expect the total loss of special status species plants and/or habitat in the developable area.	Trend: Decreasing. Special status species plant habitat in the Mojave Desert is expected to continue to decline due to human development.	Basic component (along with other vegetation).	Mitigation of special status species plants is required BLM policy.	Yes
Visual Resources	Yes	Certain	Somewhat. Visual quality of the SEZ and surrounding area is already altered.	Somewhat. Approximately 53% of viewsheds in the Mojave Desert have been altered.	Land use (human element).	Other resource mitigation that involves restoring the physical and biological integrity to the landscape may also mitigate visual resources as long as the visual design elements of form, line, color, and texture are factored into the restoration planning and design.	Visual resources must be included as a part of the site selection criteria for mitigating other biological resources that warrant habitat enhancement treatments, as a co-beneficiary of the mitigation effort. Restoration or protection of intact ecosystems can also restore or protect visual resources.

Resource/ Issue	Unavoidable Impacts?[2]	How certain is it that the unavoidable impacts will occur?	How significant are the unavoidable impacts onsite?	How significant are the unavoidable impacts of developing the Dry Lake SEZ in the region (Mojave Desert)?[3]	Role in the ecosystem?[4]	Other considerations	Are potential unavoidable impacts likely to warrant regional mitigation?
Specially Designated Areas	Maybe—for impacts to desert tortoise at the Coyote Springs ACEC. Maybe—for visual impacts to the Desert National Wildlife Refuge and other specially designated areas.	Possible—if tortoise migrate or are translocated to the Coyote Springs ACEC. Visual impacts—unknown. Lack specific assessments.	Unknown—Impacts of increasing the tortoise population in the ACEC have not been assessed. Visual impacts—unknown. Lack specific assessments.	Unknown. However, any impact that adversely affects an ACEC in its ability to support desert tortoise recovery ultimately affects the overall recovery effort. Visual impacts—unknown. Lack an assessment of the conditions and trends of visual resources as seen from other specially designated areas.	Coyote Springs ACEC: the desert tortoise is a basic component. Visual impacts to specially designated areas: land use (human element).	Possible to minimize adverse impacts onsite (in the ACEC) by extending desert tortoise fencing. Possible to minimize adverse visual impacts through onsite mitigation that reduces the degree of visual contrast from new development.	Not at this time, but may be required if additional analysis reveals an adverse impact. Unknown at this time for visual impacts. Onsite mitigation measures may be adequate for protecting the viewsheds of specially designated areas.
Military	Yes	Unlikely. Aircraft emergencies occuring over the SEZ that pose a threat to human life and/or property are rare.	Somewhat. There is an elevated risk of bodily harm to aircrew who eject and land in the area and in a solar facility. The potential for property damage to the facility could alter insurance rates.	Somewhat. Coordination with the military and possible height restrictions will address most impacts.	Land use (human element).	Difficult impact to mitigate.	No
Native American Concerns	Hydrology. Yes, if nonphotovoltaic technology is permitted. Habitat loss—yes Cultural—maybe	Unlikely for hydrology. Certain for habitat loss. Unknown for cultural resources until Class III cultural inventories are completed.	See Wildlife and Special Status Species entries in this table.	See Wildlife and Special Status Species entries in this table.	Human element.		Unknown at this time. Consultation on project applications will determine whether mitigation for Native American concerns is warranted.
Invasive/ Noxious Weeds	Maybe—if weed management plan fails.	Not likely. Onsite mitigation measures are expected to protect against the establishment and/or spread of invasive/noxious weeds.	Not particularly significant. Onsite mitigation measures are expected to minimize any impacts. Monitoring will facilitate timely discovery of infestations.	Invasive/noxious weed infestation is a problematic trend in the region. However, onsite mitigation is expected to minimize any impacts on the site, as well as to the region.	Change agent.		No, but restoration or protection of intact ecosystems will also restore or protect the ability to resist invasive species.

[1] A version of this table was presented for stakeholder review through the Dry Lake Solar Energy Zone project website in December 2012; this revised version was posted to the website in February 2013.

[2] Unavoidable impacts are those that cannot be mitigated onsite by avoidance and/or minimization. Avoidance is accomplished by imposing spatial and/or temporal restrictions. Minimization is accomplished using design features and/or best management practices.

[3] Data to determine trends were taken from the BLM Mojave Basin and Range Rapid Ecoregional Assessment.

[4] Reference the conceptual models in Appendix B.

Resource/Issue	Unavoidable Impacts?[2]	How certain is it that the unavoidable impacts will occur?	How significant are the unavoidable impacts onsite?	How significant are the unavoidable impacts of developing the Dry Lake SEZ in the region (Mojave Desert)?[3]	Role in the ecosystem?[4]	Other considerations	Are potential unavoidable impacts likely to warrant regional mitigation?
Hydrology (Water/Watershed/Water Quality)	Groundwater—maybe. Surface Hydrology—maybe. Reconfiguration of topography can alter surface hydrology.	Groundwater—unlikely. The BLM will review all applications to validate net neutral water use (i.e., groundwater purchased from holders of currently used existing senior water rights). Surface hydrology—likely.	Surface hydrology: Not especially significant. Area of very low rainfall (approximately 4 inches/year). Closed hydrologic basin.	Not particularly significant, but there is a regional decline in unaltered ephemeral stream channels.	Basic component.		Groundwater—no. Surface Hydrology—yes (indirectly as a component of the ecosystem).
Riparian	Surface Hydrology—Maybe. Reconfiguration of topography can alter surface hydrology.	Somewhat—while major riparian areas within the SEZ are designated nondevelopment areas, run-off patterns and sediment load will be altered by reconfiguration of the topography on the rest of the SEZ. Onsite mitigation measures are expected to minimize impacts.	Not especially significant; PEIS analyses show about five intermittent ephemeral stream reaches with moderate sensitivity to disturbance within the SEZ.	Not particularly significant. The occurrence of intact riparian systems is declining in the Mojave Basin and Range ecoregion.	Basic component.		No, not directly. While there may be impacts to riparian systems, preservation and/or restoration of intact ecosystems in the region that include riparian areas will slow the regional decline in intact riparian ecosystems.
Cultural	Maybe.	Low—previous Class III cultural inventories in the SEZ and vicinity indicated risk of resource loss is low.	Depends on results of Class III inventory of SEZ and if significant (eligible) sites are discovered.		Human element.	Onsite mitigation measures were determined to be adequate for addressing known cultural resources.	Not at this time. However, if significant resource values are discovered during the predevelopment survey, implementing the required protection measures as established in the memorandum of agreement may result in regional mitigation measures.

Resources/issues with no unavoidable impacts:

Acoustics
Air Quality
Environmental Justice
Fire

Hazardous Waste
Lands and Realty
Livestock Grazing
Minerals
Paleontological
Recreation (includes Travel Management Areas)

Socioeconomics
Transportation
Wild Horses and Burros
Wilderness and Lands with Wilderness Characteristics

Appendix D:

BLM Screening of Candidate Regional Mitigation Sites for the Dry Lake Solar Energy Zone

The BLM interdisciplinary team used this screening tool for evaluating and recommending candidate sites to the BLM authorized officer (see definitions for criteria categories at the end of this appendix).

#	Criteria	SEZ	Candidate Sites					Notes
		Dry Lake Solar Energy Zone	Gold Butte ACEC, Las Vegas Field Office	Mormon Mesa ACEC, Ely District and Las Vegas Field Office	Coyote Springs ACEC, Las Vegas Field Office	Piute-El Dorado ACEC, Las Vegas Field Office	Coyote Springs Enhanced	
Site Characteristics								
1	Contiguous area of site (acres)	3,471	Part A: 186,909 Part B: 119,097 Part C: 38,431	149,000	75,500	328,242	149,278 acres (mix of BLM, BLM-ACEC, and FWS Desert National Wildlife Refuge)	The size, in acres, of the candidate site.
2	For ACECs, reason for designation	n/a	see note 1				see note 6	If the candidate site encompasses land in an ACEC, this field represents the value(s) present that the ACEC was established to protect.
3	Visual Resource Management Class	Class III	Class I, II (70%), and III areas present	Class III	Class III	Class III	Class III	If the VRM class of a candidate site is of higher value than that of the SEZ, improvements provided by regional mitigation would result in improvements to the higher VRM class - no points are assigned to this characteristic.
4	Consistent with resource management plan?	n/a	√	√	√	√		
5	Same HUC 4 watershed?	Lower Colorado-Lake Mead (1501)	√	√	√	X Central Nevada Desert Basins (1606)	√	The HUC 4 watershed is used to evaluate the sites; sites not in the same HUC 4 watershed would have a fairly strong hydrologic disconnect from Dry Lake SEZ.
6	Mitigation tool (restoration/ enhancement, acquisition, banking, withdrawal, special designation, etc.)	n/a	Restoration/ enhancement	Restoration/ enhancement	Restoration/ enhancement	Restoration/ enhancement	Restoration/ enhancement, restriction of activities	The type(s) of mitigation tool that would be implemented at the site.

#	Criteria	SEZ	Candidate Sites					Notes
		Dry Lake Solar Energy Zone	Gold Butte ACEC, Las Vegas Field Office	Mormon Mesa ACEC, Ely District and Las Vegas Field Office	Coyote Springs ACEC, Las Vegas Field Office	Piute-El Dorado ACEC, Las Vegas Field Office	Coyote Springs Enhanced	

Mitigation Site Qualifying Criteria

#	Criteria	SEZ	Gold Butte ACEC	Mormon Mesa ACEC	Coyote Springs ACEC	Piute-El Dorado ACEC	Coyote Springs Enhanced	Notes
7	In SEZ ecoregion?	Mojave Basin and Range	√	√	√	√ See note 2	√	
8	In SEZ ecological subregion?	Eastern Mojave	√	√	√	√	√	
9	Meets priorities for Endangered Species Act critical habitat?	n/a	√	√	√	√	√	
10	Mitigates unavoidable impacts to "least common and most geographically restricted species?"	Desert tortoise and rosy two-toned penstemon	√	√	√	√	√	Desert tortoise habitat is present in all the candidate sites, but not necessarily rosy two-toned penstemon, which will be mitigated for using other measures (i.e., onsite seed collection prior to development and sponsorship into the Center for Plant Conservation National Collection of Rare Plants).
11	Mitigates for all or most identified unavoidable impacts that warrant regional mitigation?	Unavoidable impacts that warrant mitigation at the Dry Lake SEZ include soils, vegetation, wildlife, special-status species, and visual resources. Impacts to Native American concerns that warrant mitigation may be identified through consultation.	√	√	√	√	√	
12	Similar landscape value, ecological functionality, biological value, species, habitat types, and/or natural features?	Creosote-white bursage desert scrub vegetation community is critical resource for mitigation.	√	√	√	√	√	Site includes resources critical to meet mitigation objectives.
13	Provides adequate geographic extent?	n/a	√	√	√	√	√	Provides area for mitigation at least as large as the entire developable area of the SEZ.

#	Criteria	SEZ	Candidate Sites					Notes
		Dry Lake Solar Energy Zone	Gold Butte ACEC, Las Vegas Field Office	Mormon Mesa ACEC, Ely District and Las Vegas Field Office	Coyote Springs ACEC, Las Vegas Field Office	Piute-El Dorado ACEC, Las Vegas Field Office	Coyote Springs Enhanced	
	Stop Here For Any of the Candidate Sites That Did Not Meet One or More of the Above Qualifying Criteria							
14	Presence of unique/ valuable resources or features		√	√	√	√	√	
14a	Perennial, protected sources of water?	No	√					
14b	Unique species assemblages?	None known						
14c	Protected species and/or critical habitat?	Desert tortoise	√	√	√	√	Contiguous "highest value" tortoise habitat	
14d	Desert washes or ephemeral playas?	Avoided	√				Pahranagat Wash	
14e	Other?	Vegetation types: creosotebush, white bursage, yucca, cactus. Rare plants: rosy two-toned penstemon (*Penstemon bicolor* spp. *roseus*). Wildlife: mule deer, kit fox. Special-status species: desert tortoise, golden eagle, Gila monster, Mojave Desert sidewinder, ferruginous hawk, loggerhead shrike, Le Conte's thrasher; migratory birds. Also present: desert pavement, biologial crusts	Bighorn sheep habitat		Bighorn sheep habitat		Corridor for bighorn sheep	
15	Sources of data for the site	Final Solar PEIS, BLM interdisciplinary team, stakeholders	Southern Nevada District Office	Southern Nevada District Office	Southern Nevada District Office	Southern Nevada District Office	The Nature Conservancy	

#	Criteria	SEZ	Candidate Sites					Notes
		Dry Lake Solar Energy Zone	Gold Butte ACEC, Las Vegas Field Office	Mormon Mesa ACEC, Ely District and Las Vegas Field Office	Coyote Springs ACEC, Las Vegas Field Office	Piute-El Dorado ACEC, Las Vegas Field Office	Coyote Springs Enhanced	
Effectiveness / Additionality								
16	To what extent can the full spectrum of regional mitigation goals/objectives be met simultaneously? Use scale of 1 (low) to 5 (high).	Goals: Mitigate for impacts to desert tortoise, special status species animals and plants, visual resources, and ecosystem loss.	4	4	4	4	4	
17	How effective will the mitigation be in the context of achieving mitigation goals/objectives for conserving/ restoring ecosystem intactness? Use scale of 1 (low) to 5 (high).	n/a	5	5	5	5	5	
18	For mitigation on BLM-administered lands, mitigation consists of actions not eligible for BLM or other sources of funding.	n/a	√	√	√	√	√	
Feasibility								
19	Based on action required (e.g., restoration, BLM land management action, land acquisition, congressional action), how difficult will implementation be? Use scale of 1 (difficult) to 5 (relatively easy). See note 5.	n/a	5 (restoration)	5 (restoration)	5 (restoration)	5 (restoration)	5 (restoration, enhancement)	
20	Timeframe needed to establish site as mitigation location (estimated years).	n/a	0-1	0-1	0-1	0-1	0-1	
21	Timeframe for achieving mitigation goals and objectives from implementation (estimated years).	n/a	0-30	0-30	0-30	0-30	?	Timeframe not assesssed by The Nature Conservancy.
22	Cost estimate	n/a	Total $42,672,000 over 30 yrs ($1,422,400/yr) pooled across all 4 ACECs				$1,728/acre ($150 million)	

#	Criteria	SEZ	Candidate Sites					Notes
		Dry Lake Solar Energy Zone	Gold Butte ACEC, Las Vegas Field Office	Mormon Mesa ACEC, Ely District and Las Vegas Field Office	Coyote Springs ACEC, Las Vegas Field Office	Piute-El Dorado ACEC, Las Vegas Field Office	Coyote Springs Enhanced	
Durability								
23	How durable would the mitigation be from a timeframe and management perspective? Use scale of 1 (low) to 5 (high).	n/a	5	4	4	4	4	Rated the ACECs as having a relatively high durability (4) by virtue of being designated in the RMP for special management and because Southern Nevada District Office recommends increased law enforcement; Gold Butte rated higher because it is a site most likely to be resistant to the effects of climate change.
24	How durable would the mitigation be in the context of permanence of conservation and biodiversity protections? Use scale of 1 (low) to 5 (high).	n/a	5	4	4	4	4	
Risk								
25	What are the constraints or threats to success?	n/a	see note 3				see note 4	
26	To what extent will surrounding land uses impact mitigation success? Use scale of 1 (considerable) to 5 (low).	n/a	5	5	5	5	3	
27	What is the relative probablility of success? Use scale of 1 (low) to 5 (high).	n/a	5	5	5	5	5	
	Preliminary Ranking (see note 7)		45	43	43	40	40	

Notes:

(1) Gold Butte ACEC: Part A: desert tortoise; Part B: sensitive plants, desert bighorn sheep, desert tortoise; Part C: high-elevation relict forest stands and desert bighorn sheep habitat. Mormon Mesa ACEC: desert tortoise habitat.

Coyote Springs ACEC: functional corridors of habitat between desert tortoise recovery units.

Piute-El Dorado ACEC: desert tortoise habitat.

(2) A portion of Piute-El Dorado ACEC appears to be located in the Central Basin and Range ecoregion.

(3) Constraints include funding availability and appropriate conditions for seed germination and establishment; for Coyote Springs ACEC, a relatively short segment of the Clark, Lincoln, and White Pine Counties Groundwater Development Project pipeline and power line right-of-way (approximately 6.5 mi and 0.15 mi, respectively); and the associated water treatment facility and buried storage reservoir (approximately 75 acres total) are located within the ACEC but outside of the designated Lincoln County Conservation, Recreation, and Development Act utility corridor that runs along U.S. Route 93.

(4) Adjacent lands at risk from future development around Coyote Springs golf course which could impact groundwater and reduce conservation value; a majority of the Clark, Lincoln, and White Pine Counties Groundwater Development Project pipeline and power line right-of-way in this area are located within the designated Lincoln County Conservation, Recreation, and Development Act utility corridor that runs along U.S. Route 93, and none of the right-of-way is located within the USFWS Desert National Wildlife Refuge.

(5) For scale, consider the following: restoration, relatively easy (5); BLM land management action, not easy to moderately complicated (3-5); land acquisition, moderately complicated to not very easy (1-3); congressional action, not very easy (1).

(6) Includes part of the Coyote Springs ACEC which was established to preserve functional corridors of habitat between desert tortoise recovery units.

(7) Scores are calculated based on entries in blue-shaded cells as follows: all scaled values (i.e., ratings from 1 to 5) are summed; 1 point is added for each check mark; 2 point are deleted for each X.

Definitions for Criteria Categories

Site characterization criteria: characteristics of the site that are largely known or measureable, that determine whether the site is comparable to the SEZ site and/or is suitable for supporting effective mitigation actions.

Effectiveness/additionality criteria: factors that (1) measure how effective the actions at the mitigation site will be in terms of meeting the BLM's mitigation goals/objectives for the SEZ and (2) assess whether or not the action meets the requirement for additionality (i.e., is the site eligible for BLM or other sources of funding).

Feasibility criteria: factors that measure the degree of difficulty in terms of implementing the actions at the mitigation site, the amount of time required to successfully implement the mitigation action(s), and the total and per-acre cost of the mitigation.

Durability criteria: factors that measure the durability of the mitigation in terms of the permanence and stability of the mitigation area.

Risk criteria: factors that measure the degree to which external factors might jeopardize long-term success of the mitigation action(s).

Appendix E:

Mitigation of Visual Resource Impacts in the Dry Lake Solar Energy Zone

1.0 Introduction

Utility-scale solar development often involves a long-term commitment of relatively large areas of land and may result in substantial impacts to visual resource values. Unavoidable impacts to visual resources are those that cannot be adequately mitigated onsite by avoidance and/or by the implementation of design features meant to minimize impacts that lead to a loss or reduction in inventoried visual values. It is recognized that regional mitigation may not always be warranted for all unavoidable visual resource impacts. The BLM's interim policy, Draft Manual Section 1794, "Regional Mitigation" (referred to as the Regional Mitigation Manual throughout the rest of this appendix) outlines interim policy for taking a landscape-scale regional approach to mitigating project impacts to resources and values managed by the BLM. This interim policy guided the process developed for determining the need to mitigate visual impacts in the Dry Lake Solar Energy Zone (SEZ) at a regional level.

The process of preliminarily identifying unavoidable impacts to all resources (e.g., soils, ecological resources, cultural resources) that may warrant regional mitigation (explained in Sections 2.4.3.1 and 2.4.3.2 of this strategy) evaluates:

1. Resource condition and regional trends affecting the resource.

2. Importance placed on the resource in the land use plan.

3. Rarity, legal status, or state/national policy of the resource.

4. Resilience of the resource in the face of change and impact.

This appendix provides additional information on a strategy for considering regional mitigation to compensate for certain unavoidable impacts to visual values that may result from solar development within the Dry Lake SEZ. The criteria for preliminarily identifying unavoidable impacts to visual resource values that may warrant regional mitigation follows the same logic used for all resources outlined in the Dry Lake Solar Regional Mitigation Strategy (SRMS), but the evaluation is tailored to consider the following:

1. General regional condition of the visual resource reflected in the visual resource inventory (VRI).

2. Scarcity of the resource at the regional scale.

3. Resilience of the resource in the face of change and impact.

4. Importance placed on the resource in the land use plan.

In addition to the Regional Mitigation Manual, the process described in this appendix follows the guidance outlined in the BLM technical reference titled "Procedural Guidance

for Developing Solar Regional Mitigation Strategies" (SRMS Tech Reference), Appendix F: Mitigation of Impacts on Visual Resources. Additional sources used to develop the following include the BLM's "Visual Resource Management" Manual MS-8400, "Visual Resource Inventory" Handbook H-8410-1, and "Visual Resource Contrast Rating" Handbook H-8431-1.

2.0 Visual Resources within the Dry Lake Solar Energy Zone and the Mojave Desert Ecoregion

This appendix addresses two aspects of visual resources, which are mentioned in this strategy under 2.5.1, Background on Regional Goals:

1. Change to visual resource values within the boundary of the SEZ.

2. Change within the SEZ that would affect the visitor's scenery viewing experience from lands with legislated protection for scenery and/or landscape settings, including the following types of specially designated areas:
   a. National parks.
   b. National wildlife refuges.
   c. Wilderness areas.
   d. National scenic and historic trails.
   e. Special recreation management areas.

This appendix follows the progression of basic steps to ascertain whether regional mitigation is warranted as outlined in the SRMS Technical Reference, Section 2.4, Solar Regional Mitigation Strategy Elements (BLM forthcoming).

2.1 Define the Baseline for Assessing Unavoidable Impacts

The baseline for assessing unavoidable impacts is drawn from the impact analysis and VRIs performed for the "Final Programmatic Environmental Impact Statement (PEIS) for Solar Energy Development in Six Southwestern States" (Final Solar PEIS) (BLM and DOE 2012). The VRIs describe and quantify visual values in terms of scenic quality, public sensitivity, and distance zones (see BLM Handbook H-8410-1). Data, figures, trends, and statements of value used here were derived and extrapolated from the following VRIs for lands within the Mojave Desert ecoregion:

- Southern Nevada District.
- Ely District (Nevada).
- Palm Springs-South Coast Field Office (California).
- Barstow Field Office (California).
- Needles Field Office (California).
- Ridgecrest Field Office (California).

These VRIs include 90% of the BLM-administered lands within the Mojave Desert ecoregion. VRI data were not available for the remaining 10% of the BLM-administered lands within the Mojave Desert ecoregion. The areas not inventoried are located along the outer edges of the ecoregion in the following BLM areas of responsibility:

- Kingman Field Office (Arizona).
- Arizona Strip Field Office.
- Grand Canyon-Parashant National Monument (Arizona).
- St. George Field Office (Utah).

2.2 Regional Condition and Trends of the Visual Resource Values

The regional condition of the visual resource is extrapolated from the "scenic quality" rating evaluation for the "cultural modification" factor (see Figure 1). Cultural modification is defined as "any man-caused change in the land form, water form, vegetation, or the addition of a structure which creates a visual contrast in the basic elements (form, line, color, texture) of the naturalistic character of a landscape" (BLM Manual 8400). BLM Handbook H-8410-1 explains that cultural modifications may distract or complement the natural landscape setting and result in either a reduction in value, increase in value, or no change in value.

A review of the condition within the Mojave Desert ecoregion, based on the VRIs, indicated that 47% of the BLM-administered lands remain visually intact with no cultural modifications, or with cultural modifications present, but not contributing to or subtracting from the other scenic quality attributes.

Fifty-three percent of the ecoregion landscape contains cultural modifications that are either discordant or complementary to the landscape's scenic quality (48% of the landscape received a negative score ranging from -1 to -4, reducing the landscape's scenic quality, while 5% received a positive score).

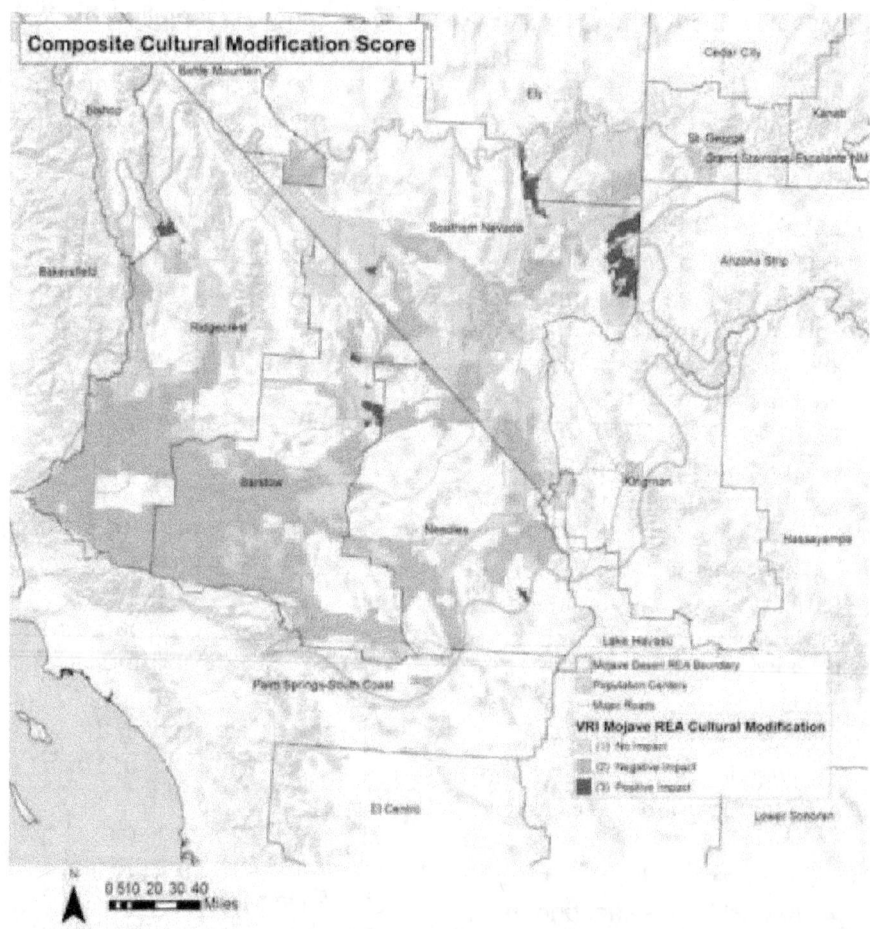

Figure 1. Composite map compiled from the visual resource inventories for cultural modifications within the Mojave Desert ecoregion.

The Dry Lake SEZ is located within Scenic Quality Rating Unit 037-Dry Lake Valley and is documented as having cultural modifications that have discordant characteristics resulting in a negative score of -1.5. The cultural modification score was subtracted from the baseline score of 7, which is the sum of the other six scenic quality evaluation key factors (see SRMS Tech Reference, Appendix F) leading to a final outcome of 5.5, which assigns a rating of Scenic Quality C.

Locating the Dry Lake SEZ within the culturally modified SQRU 037 (see Figure 2) will result in clustering new development with existing development, which will help curtail the perpetuating trend of new development sprawling into landscapes with naturalistic character. Onsite mitigation at the Dry Lake SEZ should be planned and implemented to avoid further reduction in the scenic quality.

Avoiding further reduction in the cultural modification factor could be achieved through well-planned implementation of the visual design features outlined in the Final Solar PEIS. Although solar development in the SEZ will result in increased cultural modification, thoughtful planning of the development patterns, architectural treatments, and repetition of the low visual contrasting qualities of existing and future common elements (e.g., use of Cor-Ten weathering steel transmission towers), may result in visually unifying the SEZ development with the existing scattered facilities that appear to be randomly located within the landscape. Visually integrating new and existing facilities may help create the visual impression of a well-planned industrial solar energy development that better harmonizes with the landscape setting. If well-executed, the planned development could conceivably maintain the current cultural modification score for the SEZ lands.

2.3 Scarcity

The Federal Land Policy and Management Act (FLPMA) Section 202(c)(6) requires that land use plans and revisions of land use plans "consider the relative scarcity of the values involved and the availability of alternative means (including recycling) and sites for realization of those values." The VRIs provide an assessment of three visual values (i.e., scenic quality, public sensitivity, and distance zones) and quantity of those values to determine the relative scarcity of a particular visual resource within the region.

All three visual values can be assessed for scarcity, but the principal value serving as the driver to protect scarce visual resources lies within the scenic quality value, while public sensitivity and distance zones serve as qualifiers. The inventoried visual values are measured in acres, providing information necessary for quantifying scarcity and abundance at the local and regional scale. While FLPMA does not define a quantified threshold for visual resource scarcity, or for any other resource, the assessment of scarcity is a basic statistical evaluation of the distribution of values across the landscape. The values are first evaluated independently and then in combination in the context of the VRI Class Matrix (Figure 3).

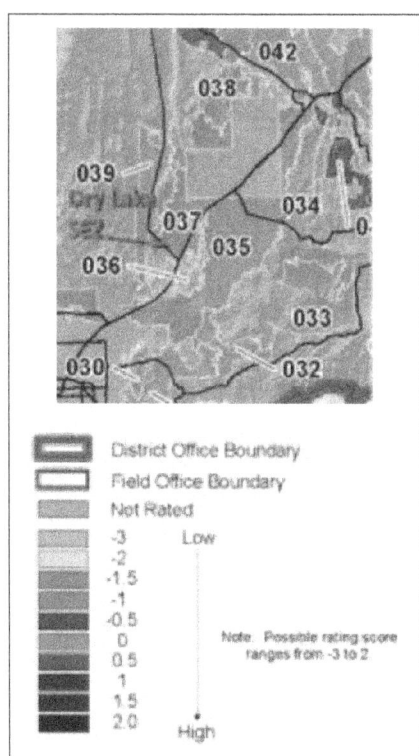

Figure 2. Scenic Quality Rating Unit 037 where the Dry Lake Solar Energy Zone is located and which has a cultural modification score of -1.5 (Southern Las Vegas Visual Resource Inventory).

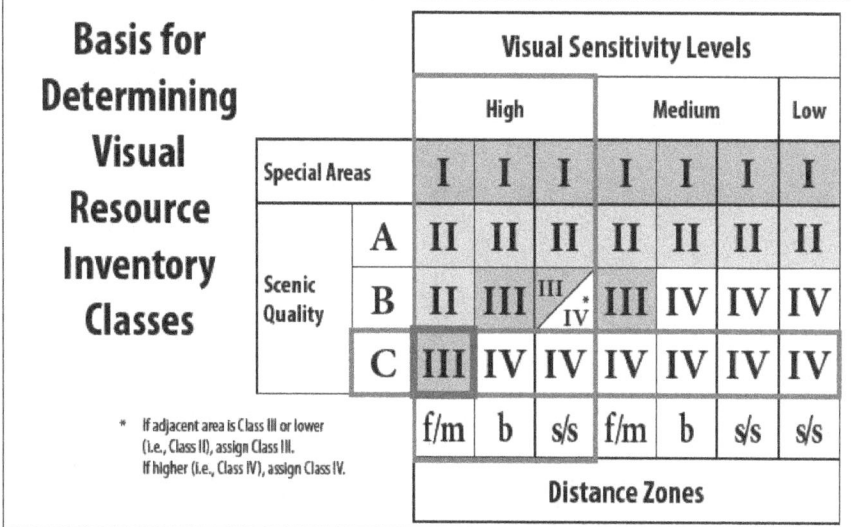

Figure 3. Visual Resource Inventory Class Assignment Matrix.

While scarcity of resources may imply worthiness for protection, in visual resources, scarcity may serve as either a value worthy of preserving or, in some circumstances, exhibit rare opportunities for development. Therefore, it is critical to review the scarcity of each visual value independently and then in combination to best understand the opportunities and constraints on development or regional mitigation.

2.3.1 Scenic Quality Scarcity

Scenic quality scarcity should be evaluated from two perspectives. First, note the scoring on the "Scenic Quality Field Inventory" BLM Form 8400-1, in which scarcity of scenic landscape features is documented. The second involves evaluating the level of scarcity within the full range of scenic quality values inventoried for the region.

2.3.1.1 Scarcity Value within the Scenic Quality Evaluation of the Visual Resource Inventory

When inventorying visual resources, scarcity is one of the seven key evaluation factors considered in the scenic quality evaluation (see Figure 4). The "scarcity factor" ranges in score from "1" for common landscapes to "5" or more for landscapes identified as "one of a kind," "unusually memorable," or "very rare". A score of 5 and above, and in some circumstances 4, should be considered scarce and should justify onsite preservation or potential regional mitigation (i.e., mitigation locations outside the area of impact).

2.3.1.2 Scarcity of Scenic Quality Values A, B, and C

Apart from the scenic quality rating unit scarcity score, a closer examination of individual visual resource value (A, B, and C) acreages and distribution can also provide insight on overall scarcity. The quantity and distribution of Scenic Quality A, B, and C acreages should be assessed and carefully examined. The distribution of these scenic quality classes within the Mojave Desert ecoregion is as follows:

1. Scenic Quality A: 653,808 acres (6.7%)

2. Scenic Quality B: 4,871,253 acres (49.7%)

3. Scenic Quality C: 4,268,449 acres (43.6%)

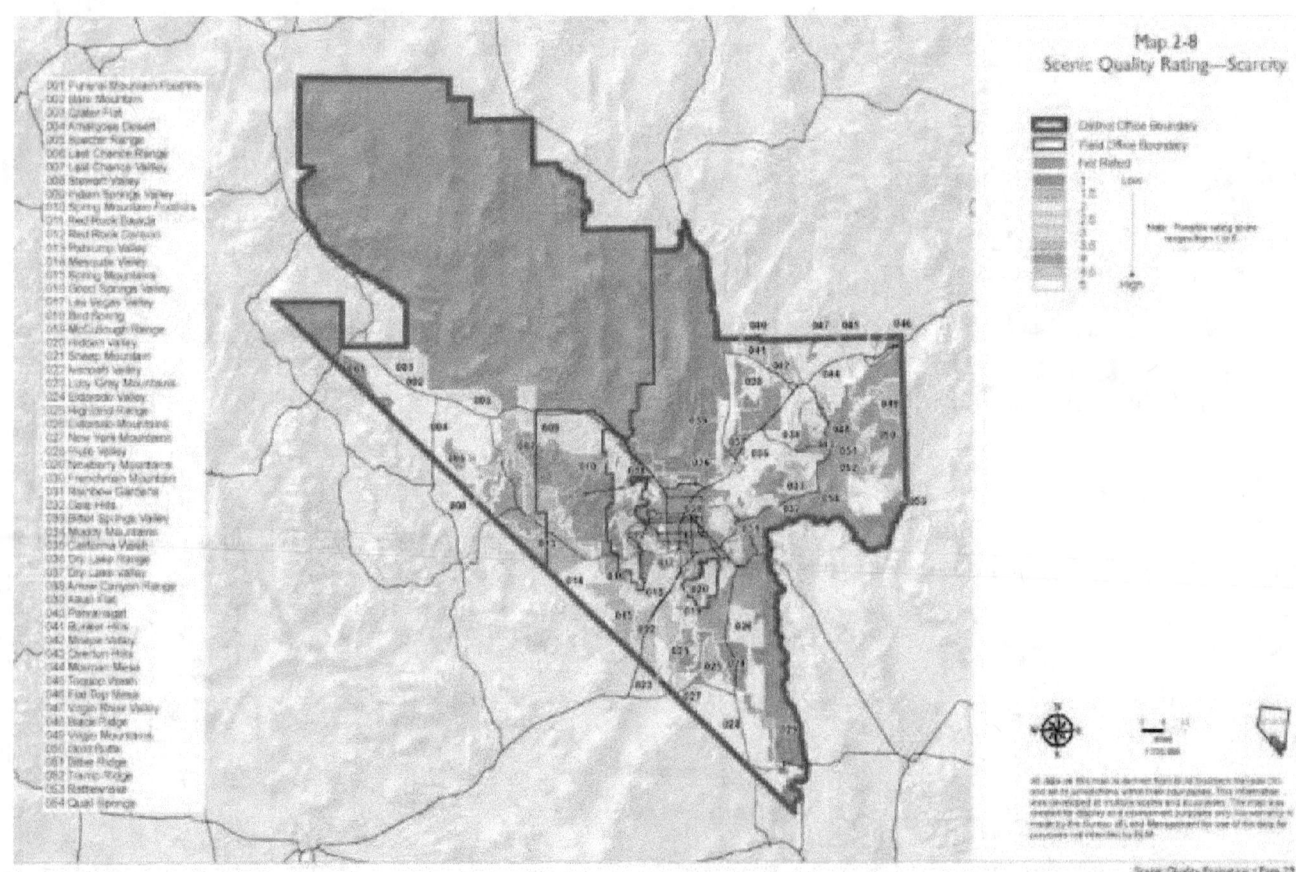

Figure 4: Example - Southern Nevada District visual resource inventory scenic quality scarcity rating map.

This distribution indicates that Scenic Quality A is scarce across the Mojave Desert ecoregion, whereas Scenic Qualities B and C are abundant. The Dry Lake SEZ is located within an area assigned a Scenic Quality C value, which indicates scarcity as a nonissue at a local and regional scale.

2.3.2 Public Sensitivity Scarcity

The Mojave Desert ecoregion public sensitivity values are:

1. High Sensitivity:
   5,840,690 acres (60%)

2. Medium Sensitivity:
   2,239,061 acres (23%)

3. Low Sensitivity:
   1,713,510 acres (17%)

The majority of the region is assigned a high public sensitivity rating in the VRI, including the location of the Dry Lake SEZ. While not scarce, this outcome indicates that the general public has a high regard for the scenic resources within these areas and that careful consideration should be given to the how solar development is visually integrated with the surrounding landscape character.

2.3.3 Distance Zone Scarcity

The Mojave Desert ecoregion distance zone values are:

1. Foreground/Middle-Ground
   7,394,810 acres (76%)

2. Background:
   633,769 acres (6%)

3. Seldom Seen:
   1,764,931 acres (18%)

The Dry Lake SEZ is located within the Foreground/Middle-Ground zone, which contains a large majority of the BLM landscape within the ecoregion. While scarcity is not a factor in respect to the distance zone, SEZ development will be within the Foreground/Middle-Ground and within close view of the public where the noticeability of visual change is highest and the visual contrasts are typically greatest.

Attention should also be drawn to the less abundant distance zones of Background and Seldom Seen landscapes. The spatial distribution of these backcountry settings may indicate a scarcity of more significance, especially when paired up with the other high visual values such as Medium to High Sensitivity and Scenic Qualities A and B.

2.3.4 Dry Lake Visual Resource Inventory Class Scarcity

VRI Classes are determined through overlaying the three inventoried values (scenic quality, sensitivity, and distance zones). The combination of the individual values assigns VRI Class II, III, or IV. The VRI Class assignments are derived from the VRI Class Matrix where the point of intersection between the three values determines the VRI Class (see Figure 5 and SRMS Tech Reference, Appendix F, for a complete explanation).

There are 21 possible combinations between the three visual values. The acreage and percent of the SEZ acreage can be determined for each of the 21 combinations of scenic quality/sensitivity/distance zones to diagrammatically illustrate their relative commonality or scarcity within the ecoregion.

Approximately 90% of the Dry Lake SEZ is inventoried as a VRI Class III, while the other 10% is VRI Class IV. The visual resource values present within the VRI Class III boundaries of the Dry Lake SEZ include Scenic Quality C, High Sensitivity, and Foreground/Middle-Ground Distance Zone (Figure 5). This particular combination of values covers 21% of the BLM acreage within the Mojave Desert ecoregion. Out of 21 possible combinations, this specific layering of values ranks as the second most abundant behind Scenic Quality B, High Sensitivity, Foreground/Middle-Ground. This outcome indicates that the Dry Lake SEZ is located within an area that has common visual values; however, it should be noted that even though the SEZ contains common visual values, there remains high public sensitivity within the highly visible foreground. Consideration for the public sensitivity to visual change within the foreground should remain a factor when making final decisions on whether visual impacts may warrant regional mitigation.

The other approximately 10% of the Dry Lake SEZ that was inventoried as VRI Class IV includes Scenic Quality C, Medium Sensitivity, and Foreground/Middle-Ground and represents 8% of the BLM acreage within the Mojave Desert Ecoregion.

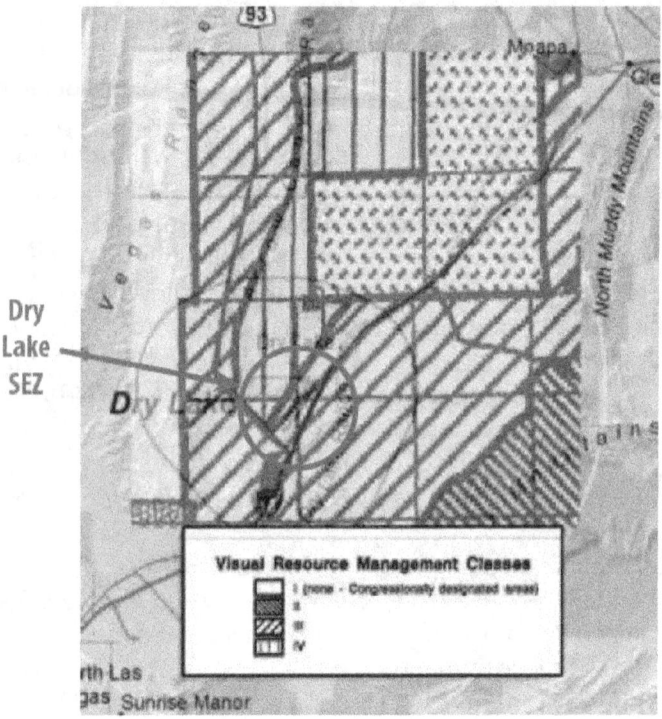

Figure 5. Graphic illustration of the 1998 Las Vegas RMP visual resources management map over the Dry Lake Solar Energy Zone visual resource inventory map (Nevada Test Site).

2.4 Visual Resource Resiliency

There are two aspects measured for visual resource resilience (see SRMS Technical Reference, Appendix F, for more information on determining visual resource resiliency):

1. Ability of the landscape to visually absorb the visual change imposed by development within the SEZ.

2. Ability of the landscape to visually return to a naturalized intact appearance after decommissioning the SEZ operation.

The Dry Lake SEZ is within the Foreground/Middle-Ground and immediately contiguous to two high-volume highways (U.S. Route 93 and Interstate 15) from where the public would commonly view the landscape. The large scale of development within the SEZ in proximity of the two highways would likely be consistent with only the VRM Class IV objective. The spatial orientation of the Dry Lake SEZ to the casual observer would lead to the conclusion that the SEZ has no visual resilience. The visual resilience at decommissioning would be consistent with resilience determination for the ecological resources of the Mojave Desert ecoregion, which has been determined to be low resilience.

2.5 Importance Placed on the Resource in the Land Use Plan

VRM Class designations are made in the land use plan or resource management plan, which prescribes the allowable degree of visual contrast that may be created by land use actions on BLM-administered lands, including energy development activities. These decisions establish the VRM Class objectives for a given parcel of BLM-administered lands and are legally binding land use decisions requiring conformance by all land use actions potentially affecting the visual characteristics of the landscape. Proposed land use actions that are found to be out of conformance with the VRM objectives are either denied approval, modified until they demonstrate conformance, or require a land use plan amendment to change the VRM objectives for the lands where the land use actions are proposed.

The "Proposed Las Vegas Resource Management Plan and Final Environmental Impact Statement" (Las Vegas RMP) (BLM 1998) designated the Dry Lake SEZ area as VRM Class III and VRM Class IV (see Figure 5). The VRM Class III allocation sits within the eastern half of the SEZ and is bordered by and runs parallel to Interstate 15. The VRM Class III area is also flanked by U.S. Route 93 on the southern perimeter of the SEZ. The VRM Class IV allocation is located west of the VRM Class III area away from Interstate 15, but flanked along U.S. Route 93.

Given the proximity of the SEZ to the heavily traveled Interstate 15 and U.S. Route 93, it is likely that solar development within the SEZ would not conform to the VRM Class III objective. The VRM Class III objective specifies that development may be seen and may attract visual attention, but it must not visually dominate the landscape.

The character and scale of facilities and features commonly associated with solar development located within the foreground proximity of the highways would likely visually dominate the landscape and, thus, would not conform with VRM Class III requirements. This assumption would need to be confirmed through the BLM's formal process for determining VRM Class objective conformance using the Visual Contrast Rating System (see BLM Handbook H-8431-1). If found to be out of conformance with the VRM Class III objective, the Las Vegas RMP would need to be amended so that the entire area available for solar energy development within the SEZ is VRM Class IV, in order to properly permit the proposed actions; the VRM Class IV objective permits major modification of the landscape that may dominate views of the project area.

Amending the land use plan implies impacting a resource in a manner that was not anticipated by the prior land use planning process, thereby modifying the balance among the decisions made on how to best manage the visual values in relation to other competing resource values. Impacting this resource to a greater degree than previously planned may warrant replacing the impaired values in suitable areas outside of the impact area of the proposed action in order to maintain a balanced approach to managing the visual resources.

2.6 Regional Visual Mitigation Goals and Objectives

The following Dry Lake SEZ visual regional mitigation goals and objectives were developed using Appendix F from the SRMS Tech Reference (BLM forthcoming). They are high-level goals and objectives based on the outcome of applying the procedures:

- **Goal:** Restore and/or protect the visual resource values altered by development of the SEZ (taking into account the existing condition of visual resource values in the Dry Lake SEZ).

- **Objective:** Restore and/or protect visual resource values proportionate to expected impacts in concert with ecosystem restoration.

These goals and objectives should be carried forward and also serve as a framework for identifying mitigation location-specific visual resource goals and objectives.

2.6.1 Summary of the Basis for Visual Resource Regional Mitigation Recommendation

Considering the cross-section between the general condition and trend of the visual values reflected in the VRI; scarcity of the visual values at the regional scale; resilience in the face of change; and importance placed on the resource in the land use plan, the following conclusions were made as a result of the aforementioned goal and objective in 2.6:

1. **General condition and trend of the visual values reflected in the VRI.** The VRI illustrates a visual condition of the Mojave Desert ecoregion as a landscape that is 53% culturally modified (visually changed). Given the direction of national policy promoting the development of renewable energy sources on BLM-administered lands, combined with federal and state incentives for encouraging the energy industry to invest in new renewable energy projects, it is reasonable to expect a trend toward expanded visual change of the BLM-administered public lands. The Dry Lake SEZ is located within a landscape that is already modified (see Figure 6); however, the degree of visual change would significantly increase due to solar development.

Figure 6. Viewing northwest into the Dry Lake Solar Energy Zone from U.S. Route 93

2. **Importance placed on the resource in the land use plan.** Development within the SEZ will likely not conform to the current Las Vegas RMP VRM Class III objective and will need amending to allow for a greater degree of visual change. The SEZ will likely become the dominant unnatural visual feature within the Dry Lake Valley as new solar energy facilities are constructed over the life of the SEZ. This degree of visual change was not anticipated in the Las Vegas RMP (BLM 1998) and will necessitate a rebalancing of the management of visual resource values.

3. **Scarcity of the visual values at the regional scale.** The SEZ is located within an area inventoried as Scenic Quality C and represents 43% percent of the Mojave Desert ecoregion, which would be considered a regionally common visual value. However, it is paired with high public sensitivity and is within the visually exposed Foreground/Middle-Ground distance zone.

4. **Resilience in the face of change.** The landscape character where the SEZ is located is not conducive to visually absorbing the proposed scale of solar development from where people commonly view the landscape, leading to the conclusion that there would be no resiliency while the SEZ is fully operational. The landscape the SEZ is located within is also very difficult to successfully revegetate. A long-term visual footprint will likely be left behind and remain over a significant period of time after the SEZ is decommissioned, indicating a low visual resilience.

It is recommended that the values lost be recovered elsewhere through regional mitigation, in consideration of (1) the present and future change to the landscape's natural character; (2) the SEZ being located in the foreground of a visually sensitive landscape; (3) the visual change anticipated to occur within the SEZ being more visually dominant than what was foreseen within the Las Vegas RMP; and (4) the low resilience of the landscape during SEZ operation and post-decommissioning. When factoring the commonality of Scenic Quality C and an indicator of low scenic quality, the recommendation for achieving the goal for restoring and/or protecting the visual resource values altered by development of the SEZ should be pursued through a combined approach, incorporating the stated visual objective into the planning and implementation of the regional mitigation goals and objectives for ecosystem restoration.

This strategy identifies the Gold Butte Area of Critical Environmental Concern (ACEC) as the recommended location for regional mitigation of ecological resource impacts. The visual values within the Gold Butte ACEC are higher than those of the Dry Lake SEZ, which provides opportunity for enhancement or preservation of an area regarded as having high visual resource value in combination with high ecological resource value.

2.6.2 Recommended Mitigation Location - Gold Butte Area Visual Resource Values

The visual resource regional mitigation objective calls to "restore and/or protect visual resource values proportionate to expected impacts." Offsetting expected impacts that are proportionate implies an opportunity for making acreage adjustments if the resource value lost is replaced with resources of higher value (see SRMS Tech Reference, Appendix F).

If ecological restoration and preservation activities were to occur at the Gold Butte ACEC, examination of the visual resource values inventoried within the ACEC will provide insight on locations and will also lead to a combined opportunity for recovering visual values that are equal to or greater in value to those reduced at the Dry Lake SEZ. These locations would also likely have an increase in public benefit.

2.6.2.1 Visual Resource Inventory Classes.

There is a mix of VRI Class I, II, and III within the Gold Butte ACEC, with VRI Class II representing approximately 70 percent of the area (Figure 7). The Dry Lake SEZ is located within a VRI Class III and IV area. The majority of the Gold Butte ACEC has higher visual resource values indicating that any resource restoration that visually complements the landscape will likely have a higher public benefit in exchange for the reduction in visual values at the Dry Lake SEZ.

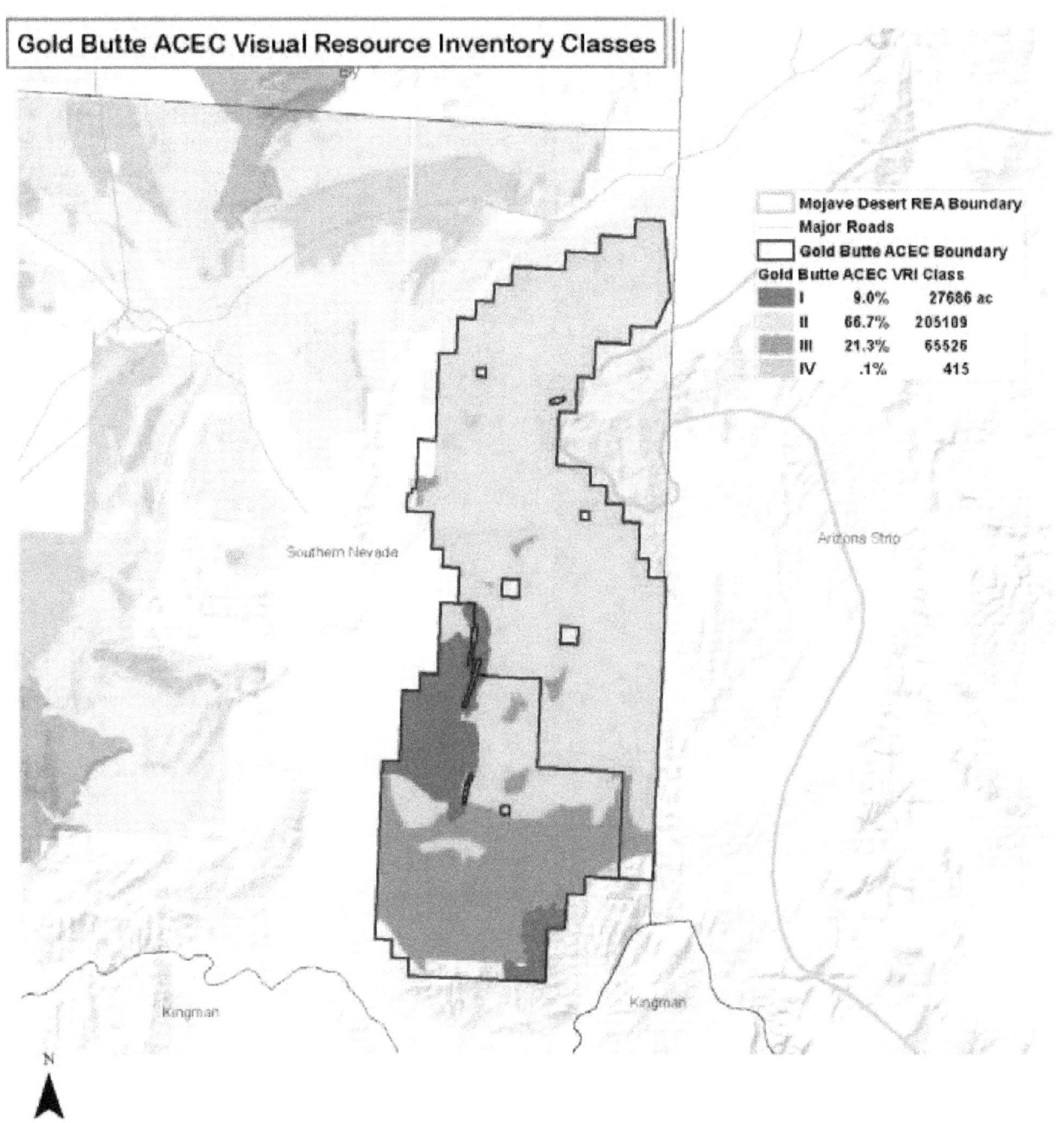

Figure 7. BLM Southern Nevada District visual resource inventory class assignment map.

Scenic Quality. Distribution of scenic quality within the Gold Butte ACEC is:

- Scenic Quality A: Approximately 60%

- Scenic Quality B: Approximately 30%

- Scenic Quality C: 0% (scenic quality for the Dry Lake SEZ area)

- Not inventoried, but within VRI Class I (wilderness area): Approximately 10%

The mix of scenic quality within the Gold Butte ACEC (Figure 8) is of higher value than what is present at the Dry Lake SEZ indicating that any resource restoration that visually complements the landscape will likely have a higher public benefit in exchange for the reduction in scenic quality at the Dry Lake SEZ.

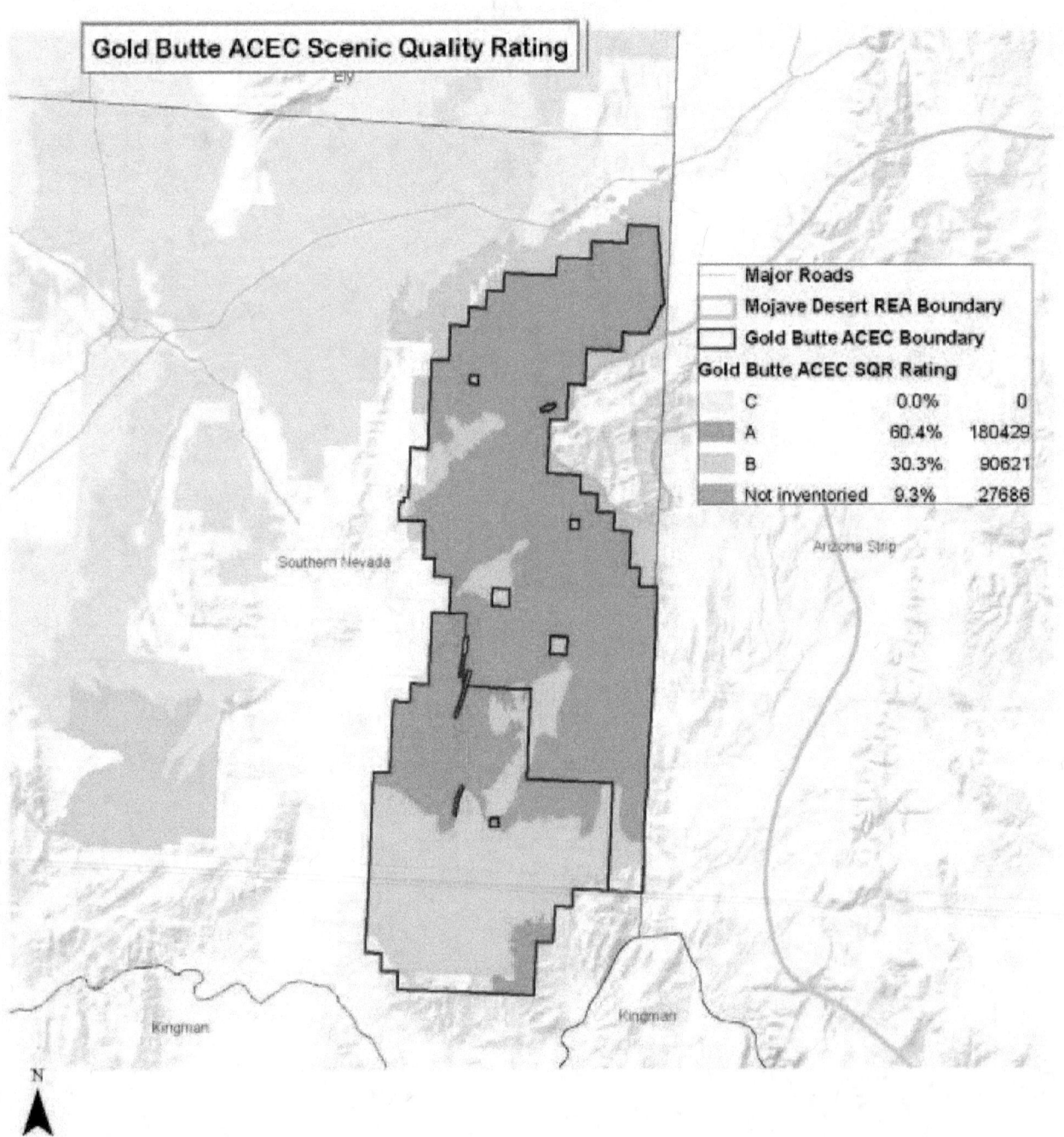

Figure 8. BLM Southern Nevada District scenic quality rating map illustrating values within the Gold Butte Area of Critical Environmental Concern.

Sensitivity. Distribution of sensitivity level within the Gold Butte ACEC is:

- High Sensitivity: Approximately 80% (public sensitivity for the Dry Lake SEZ area)

- Medium Sensitivity: 0%

- Low Sensitivity: Approximately 11%

The majority of the Gold Butte ACEC is equal to the public sensitivity level present at the Dry Lake SEZ. Ecological restoration or preservation activities should be located within the Gold Butte areas inventoried as having high public sensitivity for scenic quality and

avoid the 11% of the Gold Butte ACEC attributed to having medium and low public sensitivity (Figure 9). Ecological resource restoration that visually complements the landscape within the 80% area assigned high public sensitivity will likely have an equal public benefit in exchange for the reduction to the sensitivity value at the Dry Lake SEZ.

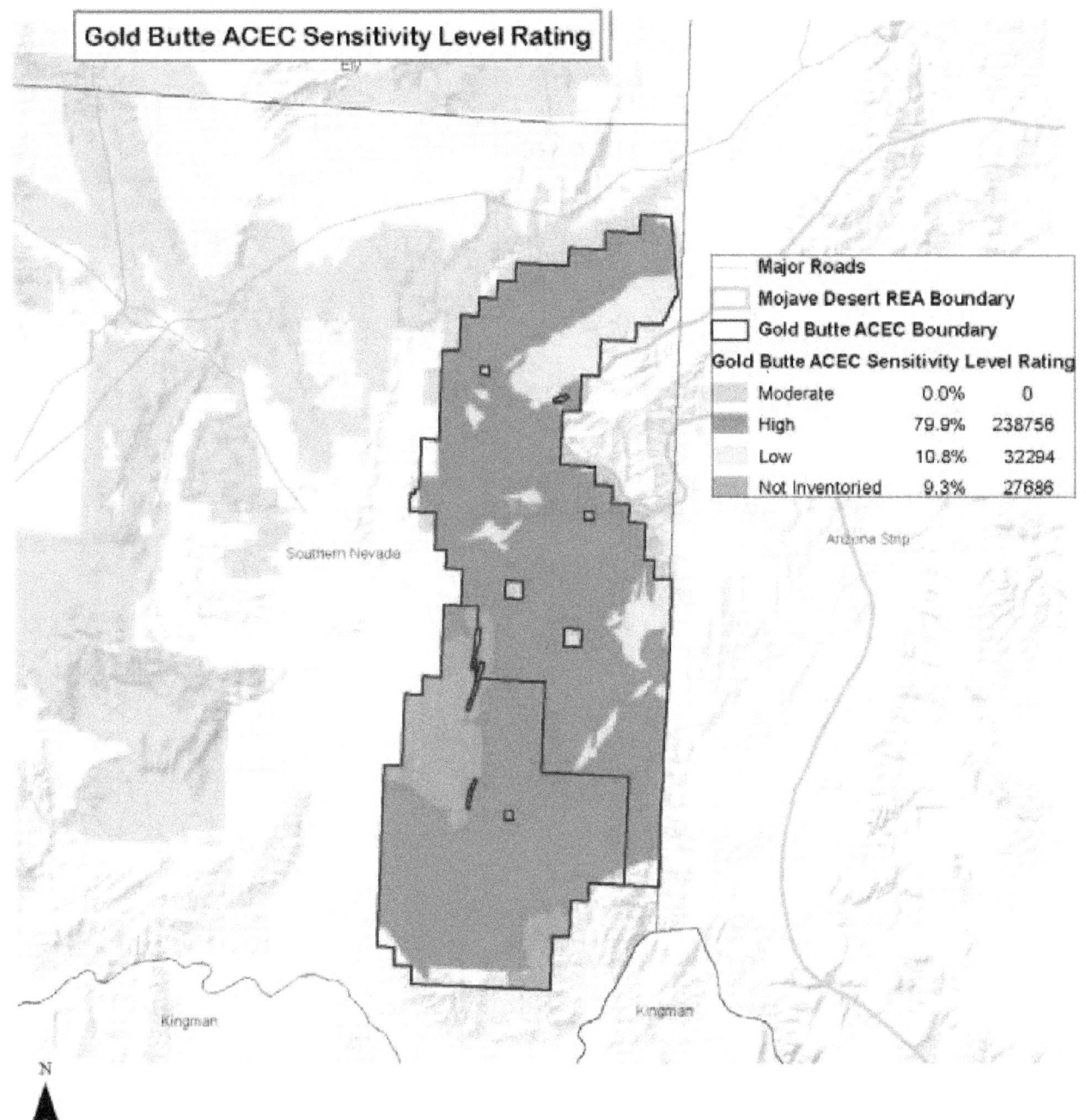

Figure 9. BLM Southern Nevada District visual resource inventory sensitivity level rating map illustrating values within the Gold Butte Area of Critical Environmental Concern.

Distance Zone. Fifty-nine percent of the Gold Butte ACEC is within the Foreground/Middle-Ground Distance Zone (Figure 10), which is the same as the Dry Lake SEZ. However, it is worth noting that 41% of the acreage inventoried within the Background and Seldom Seen Distance Zones represents a scarcer 24% of the inventoried landscape at the regional scale. Given the scarce nature of these backcountry landscape settings, ecological restoration that complements the landscapes naturalistic character will likely have an equal or greater public benefit within any of the distance zones that are paired with high sensitivity.

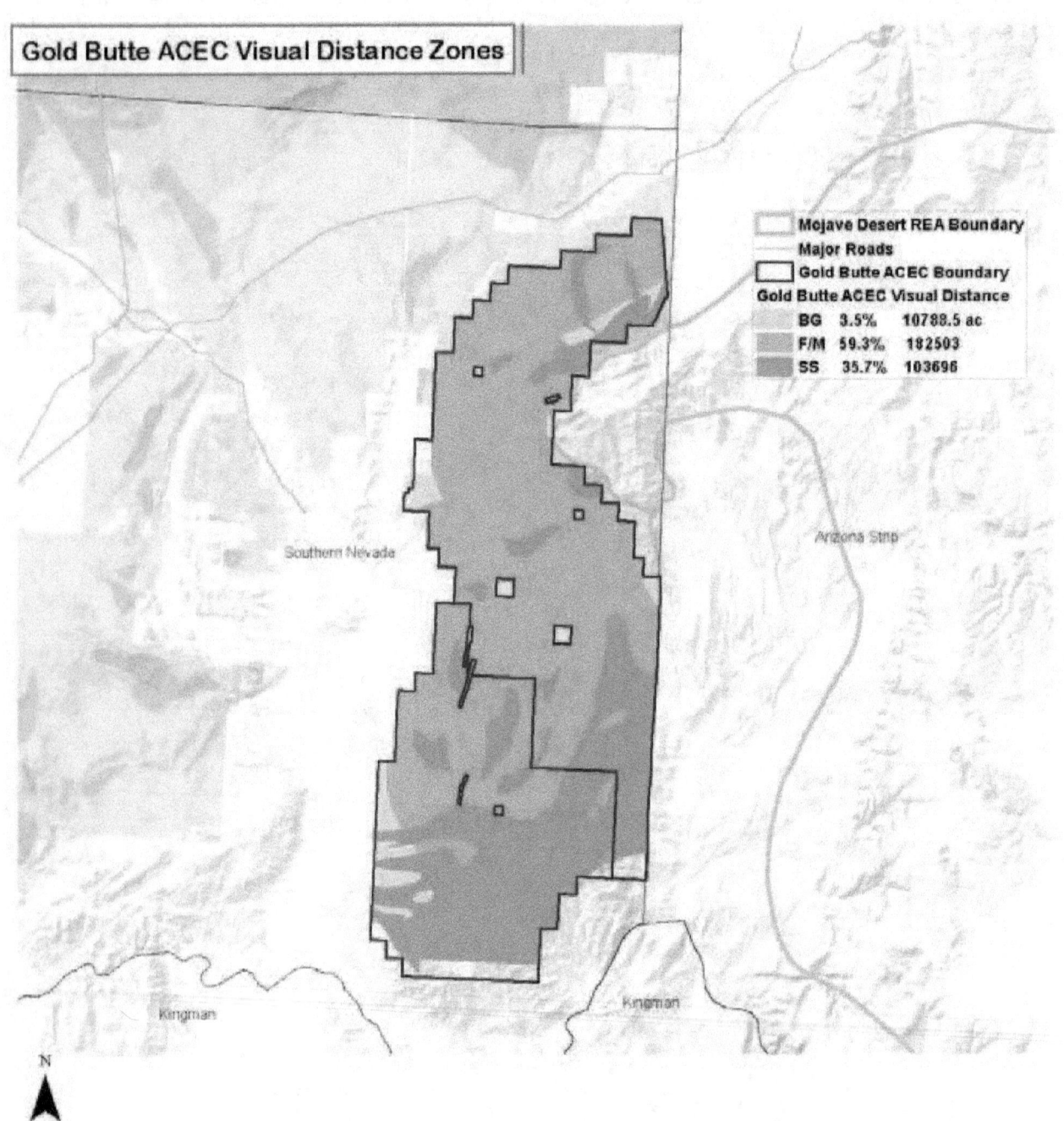

Figure 10. BLM Southern Nevada District visual resource inventory distance zone map.

VRM Class Objectives: The majority of the Gold Butte ACEC is designated for management under VRM Class II (Figure 11): retention of the natural visual characteristics of the landscape with minimal visual change. This VRM Class is more protective of visual values than those at the Dry Lake SEZ, which is currently managed as VRM Classes III and IV.

Southern Nevada District			
Inventoried Lands	3455871	District Total Acres	9793563
Visual Resource Management Classes			
	Total Acres	% of Inventoried Lands w DRECP	% of District
I	149842	4%	2%
II	942771	27%	10%
III	1802511	52%	18%
IV	560746	16%	6%
	3455871	100.0%	35.3%

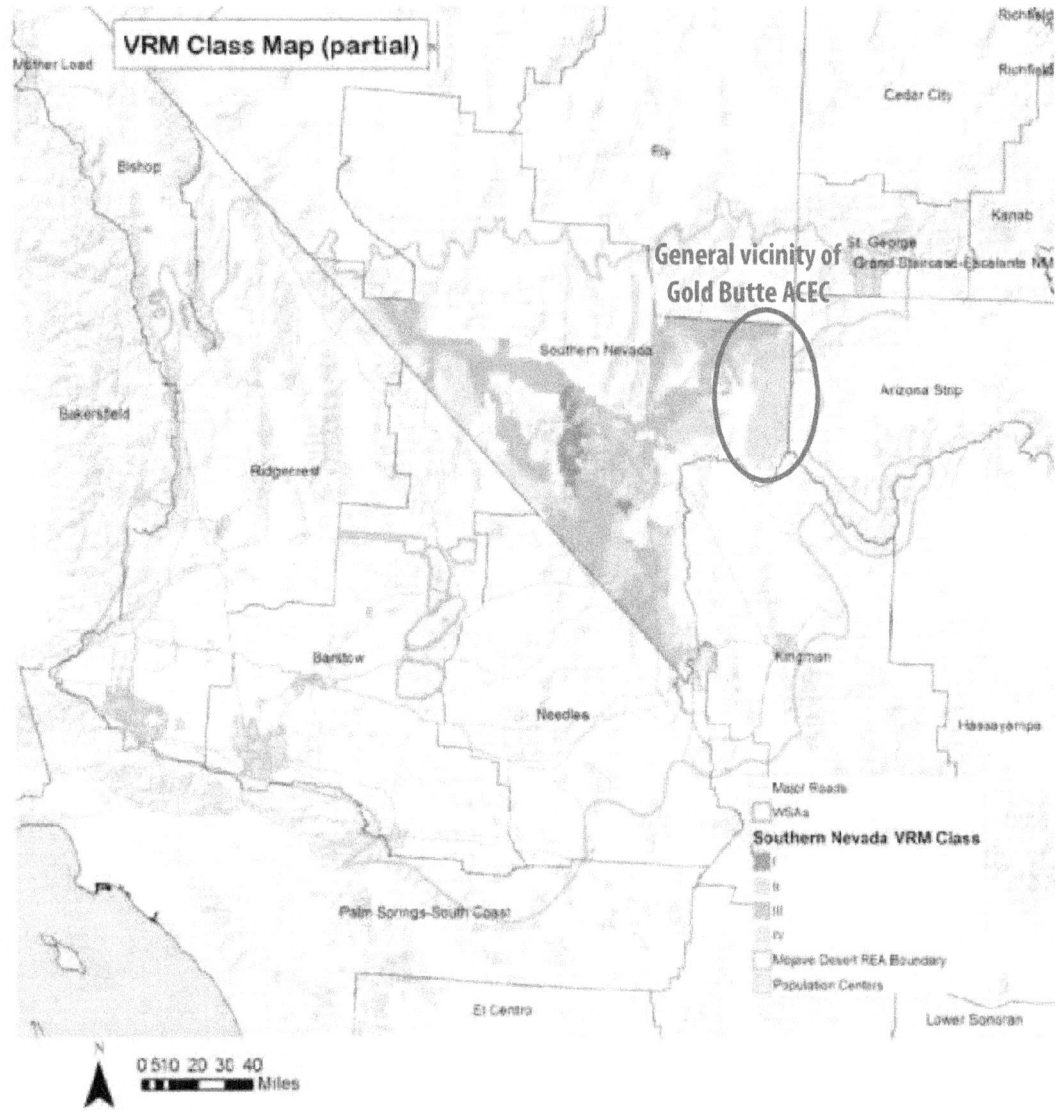

Figure 11. Visual Resource Management Classes throughout southern Nevada, including the Gold Butte Area of Critical Environmental Concern.

2.6.2.2 Visual Resource Regional Mitigation Recommendations

In concert with ecological mitigation, specifics of the visual resource mitigation recommendations are:

As the Las Vegas RMP is amended from a VRM Class III to a VRM Class IV within the Dry Lake SEZ area, also consider amending the VRM Classes within the Gold Butte ACEC involving restoration and/or protection of ecological resources from a VRM Class II to a VRM Class I—preservation of the visual resource value to protect the investment, outcome, and integrity of the ecological and visual regional mitigation actions.

If the ecological mitigation includes surface restoration, then sound visual design practices should be included as a part of the restoration planning, with the participation of the Southern Nevada District Office VRM lead (see the 2013 edition of "Best Management Practices for Reducing Visual Impacts of Renewable Energy Facilities on BLM-Administered Lands," available at http://www.blm.gov/style/medialib/blm/wo/MINERALS__REALTY__AND_RESOURCE_PROTECTION_/energy/renewable_references.Par.1568.File.dat/RenewableEnergyVisualImpacts_BMPs.pdf).

Ecological resource restoration plans should demonstrate the visual resource benefits that will be accomplished. The BLM's visual contrast rating process should be used along with descriptive narrative to demonstrate how the improvements will reflect enhanced scenic resource values within the VRI. The inventory should then be updated reflecting the positive change. The VRI demonstrates the opportunity to replace the values reduced at the Dry Lake SEZ by restoring or protecting higher values in the Gold Butte ACEC that would have greater public benefit.

2.7 Specially Designated Areas

As discussed in 2.0 of this appendix, a second consideration of unavoidable visual resource impact is to evaluate how the change within the SEZ will affect important viewsheds from lands with legislated protection for scenery and/or landscape settings, which may include, but are not limited to, the following specially designated areas:

a. National parks.
b. National wildlife refuges.
c. Wilderness areas.
d. National scenic and historic trails.
e. Special recreation management areas.

2.7.1 Dry Lake Solar Energy Zone Development Visibility from Nearby Specially Designated Areas

For the Final Solar PEIS, a preliminary analysis was conducted of the potential contrasts that might be created by solar development in the SEZ, as seen from specially designated areas that are visible from and within 25 mi of the SEZ. The analysis was conducted by constructing virtual computer models of the most visually impacting solar development technology (solar power towers) located within the Dry Lake SEZ.

The determination of unavoidable visual impacts is based on the Final Solar PEIS analysis and further evaluates those specially designated areas listed in the Final Solar PEIS as having moderate or strong visual contrast. The goal is to preliminarily identify if these impacts are unavoidable and, if so, if they may warrant further mitigation.

For the Dry Lake SEZ, the specially designated areas of concern include:

1. The Desert National Wildlife Refuge.

2. Old Spanish National Historic Trail.

3. Arrow Canyon Wilderness.

4. Nellis Dunes Special Recreation Management Area.

An exercise was conducted using Google Earth to:

• Reevaluate the impacted viewshed as delineated in the Final Solar PEIS.

• Identify potential places where people may be found recreating or conducting other activities within the affected viewshed.

• Evaluate the full field of view from locations where people are likely to view the SEZ.

• Evaluate the influence of the Visual Contrast Rating System 10 environmental factors (see BLM Handbook H-8431-1, II.D.2.b) on the degree of impact on specially designated area observers.

2.7.2 Specially Designated Area Unavoidable Impact Visual Impact Findings

2.7.2.1 Desert National Wildlife Refuge

The evaluation concluded that the Dry Lake SEZ is not within view from locations observers are known to be within the Desert National Wildlife Refuge. According to information provided by the

Desert National Wildlife Refuge, the majority of refuge visitation originates at the visitor center, with visitors accessing other areas of interest using the refuge's network of roads and trails. Views of the Dry Lake SEZ from the refuge's visitor center and network of roads and trails are obstructed by either the Sheep Range and/or the Las Vegas Range, which are west of the SEZ.

2.7.2.2 Old Spanish National Historic Trail

According to the BLM Pahrump Field Office archaeologist, the Old Spanish National Historic Trail is east of the Dry Lake SEZ and lies within the Dry Lake Range. The trail roughly runs parallel to Interstate 15 with views of the Dry Lake SEZ being obstructed by topography within the Dry Lake Range.

2.7.2.3 Arrow Canyon Wilderness Area

The areas within the Arrow Canyon Wilderness known to have high visitation include the slot canyons from which the development within the SEZ will not be visible. Nevertheless, it is likely that dispersed recreation activities will draw observers to higher elevations that overlook the Dry Lake valley.

The Final Solar PEIS viewshed analysis illustrates an estimated distance range of 9 to 22 mi from Arrow Canyon to the Dry Lake SEZ, with 4% percent (1,011 acres) of the total area of the Arrow Canyon Wilderness Area as having unobstructed views of the SEZ within the 5 to 15 mile range, with another 1% of the area (204 acres) within the 15 to 25 mile range. While views of the solar energy development may be seen, it is unlikely that the visual dominance will be greater than a VRM Class III objective (moderate levels of change may be seen and draw the attention of the casual observer, but the change does not dominate the landscape). This would be a worst case scenario from the closer proximities to the Dry Lake SEZ. The exposure within these areas is very intermittent.

The SEZ is visible from a very small portion of the Arrow Canyon Wilderness, and where visible, impacts from solar development within the SEZ are expected to be low; therefore, regional mitigation is not warranted.

2.7.2.4 Nellis Dunes Special Recreation Management Area

The Nellis Dunes Special Recreation Management Area is a popular off-highway vehicle area. The SEZ is visible from 412 acres (5%) of the Nellis Dunes, and where visible, impacts from solar development within the SEZ are expected to be negligible; therefore, regional mitigation is not warranted.

2.7.2.5 Conclusions

Unavoidable visual impacts to the specially designated areas are low with no recommendations for regional mitigation.

www.ingramcontent.com/pod-product-compliance
Lightning Source LLC
Chambersburg PA
CBHW052008280526
45793CB00005B/891